The Secrets of Silk

From the Myths and Legends
to the Middle Ages

Priscilla Lowry

i

St John's Press, London
2003

First published in the United Kingdom in 2003 by
St John's Press, London
16 Primrose Gardens, Hampstead
London NW3 4TN

Email: silkroad16@priscillalowrysilks.co.uk
or silkroad16@aol.com
Website www. priscillalowrysilks.co.uk

ISBN 0-9544140-0-4

British Library Cataloguing-in-Publication Data
A catalogue record for this book is available from the British Library

Cover illustration: The Lady of the Silkworms.

Contents

Acknowledgements

Many people have contributed to the joy of putting this book together. In particular I am indebited to the fine scholarship of many textile scholars, librarians and researchers. I am also very grateful to my friends and colleagues in the International Silk Association. To all the members of the Spinners, Dyers and Weavers, Embroiderers, Quilters, Lacemakers, Knitters, Felt and Braid makers I add my very special thanks. Your interest and encouragement has been a joy and delight and a constant source of inspiration to me. My thanks also, to Fiona Nisbet, Gaynor and Dave Thorp, Johnny Azkanazi, Robert Taylor, Judy and Bill Wilson and my sister Leone Paget for their generous help and encouragement. In particular I am greatly indebited to my editors, Christine Bachmann and Suse Coon. Finally my thanks to my family for their loving support and to whom this, the first of three volumes is dedicated.

Priscilla Lowry
London 2003

Introduction

At last the Secrets of Silk can be revealed! This book draws together the myths and legends and stories of high adventure, hardship and greed as this precious fabric traveled over the Old Silk Road. Its arrival in the West took Byzantium and Rome by storm and Marco Polo recorded just how widespread silk was in Mongol China at the time of Kublai Khan. In Britain, plain silk fabrics were exquisitely over embroidered to make priceless garments for the Church and Court. The London silkwomen conducted their businesses with both the help and hindrance of the powerful guildsmen. A constant thread throughout the whole story is the use, power and impact of silk in fashion.

There is something for everyone in the story of silk, whether your interest is in textiles, art, design, embroidery, medieval history, travel, economics or fashion. This book concludes with an extensive glossary, bibliography and a practical section on spinning silk.

帝元妃西陵氏 きうていのけんびせいりゃうし

The lady of the Silkworms, the Lady Si Ling-shi, standing serenely in front of
round wicker trays of silkworms feeding on mulberry leaves.
With kind permission of Robert Gooden, Lullingstone Silk Farm.

Chapter 1
Myths and Legends

In the Beginning:
The Lady of the Silkworms

In ancient times and in a society where the written word was available only to the chosen few, imaginative stories could embroider and flesh out barely understood facts. Myths and legends could hide the truth and keep a secret. Many of the best stories had a beautiful princess, a little magic, and an exotic tale to tell.

Back in the mists of time, the emperor Fo Xi (2677-2597 BC) was believed to have ruled China. Some say he discovered the secrets of silk, but usually Si Ling-shi (Lei-tze or Lady Xi-ling) is given the credit. She was the principal wife of the Yellow Emperor, Shih Huang-ti, who ruled China between 259 and 210 BC. Some Chinese legends say Si Ling-shi was really his concubine and other sources say she was his fourteen year old daughter. Most legends describe her as the Lady of the Silkworms or the Goddess of Silk and all agree that she was beautiful.

According to the legend, the beautiful princess was walking in the palace gardens with her ladies. Set out under a mulberry tree

Names for Silk

There is a long history of confusion about the names for China and silk. Some people called China, Sinae or Thinae, the Greeks and Romans called it Seres or Serica. The Roman writer Cosmas Indicopleusts, early in the sixth century AD, when he mentions China, calls it Tzinista, but he was not too sure and concluded that '... further than Tzinista, there is neither navigation nor an inhabited land.' Sanskrit writings also refer to Cina, from the name for the Qin dynasty, from which China is derived, Qin being in the north and Cathay being in the south. According to Theophanus of Byzantium (c750-817 AD), sericulture was introduced by a Persian who came from the land of Seres. The name possibly comes from ser, the central Asian word for yellow, the colour associated with the Chinese Imperial court. Every country has its own word for silk: The Chinese call it Si, South China used See or Szu, the Koreans Soi, and the nomads of Central Asia called it Sir, Sirghe or Sirkek. The Jews sometimes call their exquisite silk fabric Sherikoth, while the Arabs called it Saraqa. In the west the Latin text uses Sericum, French Soie, German Seide and English Silk.

Bombyx mori silk moth on a mulberry leaf.
With kind permission of Robert Gooden, Lullingstone Silk Farm.

was a little brazier, heating water to make tea. As she passed by, a silk cocoon dropped from the mulberry tree into the bowl of hot water. She picked up a chopstick and tried to scoop out the cocoon and she found a single strand of glistening silk attached. As she drew the silk out further and further, she marveled at its length and fineness. She looked in delight at the fragile shimmering silk and wondered if it could be woven and made into a beautiful soft gown, unique and precious and unlike any garment she had ever worn before. She started to imagine what it would feel like, to be clothed in a cobweb of silken cloth. She realized then that she had discovered the first secret of silk. It was hot water that dissolved the sericin the gummy substance holding the cocoon and fibres together and now the fibres were free to unwind as a continuous thread.

Si Ling-shi knew that silkworms ate mulberry leaves, she had seen them on the trees. She knew that they spun a cocoon before turning into a moth that laid eggs that would hatch into silkworms. But, until that time, it was not known if the cocoon itself had any value or if the silk could be unwound. One single strand was too thin to be easily managed on its own, but the fine silk filaments of half a dozen cocoons, softened by hot water, could be drawn off together and wound into a skein to dye, weave or transport. The discovery of how to make it into a thicker and more usable thread was the second secret of silk.

This glossy, continuous thread was quite unlike cotton or wool, with their short fibres that needed to be handspun and twisted together to make a usable yarn. Silk was smooth and strong, ideal for weaving into exquisite precious fabrics. Si Ling-shi is also credited with the discovery of weaving, but this is unlikely because weaving had already been practiced for many centuries. In ancient China, the Emperor claimed all discoveries, so it is not surprising that the invention of silk weaving was attributed to his wife, the Empress.

Si Ling-shi was called the Lady of the Silkworms and honoured with rituals and sacrifices. Court regulations decreed that the Empress and her ladies would perform a solemn ceremony to encourage the growing of silk. This ritual was timed to coincide with the fresh spring growth of leaves on the mulberry trees in the third month of the lunar year. The Empress and royal concubines prepared themselves by withdrawing from the court, fasting and offering sacrifices. The ladies then rode in horse-drawn carriages in a grand procession to the Temple of the Silkworms on the north-

Mulberry Tree. Morus alba *the preferred species and* Morus nigra, *vary in height from a bush to a tall tree.*

eastern shore of Lake Bei. They were accompanied by thousands of horsemen carrying dragon banners and colourful silk pennons. There is an account of this annual ritual in the Book of Sericulture, the Qin Guan's Can Shu, written in 1090 AD and also in the Songshu, the Book of the Song Dynasty (960-1279) which maintains that this complex ritual was first performed in 1119. The ritual and procession continued each year until the fall of the Qing Dynasty in 1911. The Hall of Imperial Silkworms with the Altar of Silkworms were situated within the Forbidden City, and this area, called Beihei, is now a children's park.

Some Chinese communities have their own folk tales to explain the origin of silk. The people of Sichuan honoured a god-king called Cancong who distributed several thousand golden silkworms to his people. Cancong means 'a silkworm cluster' and his subjects believed they were the first to wear silk. He apparently always wore green, and is known as 'the god in green'.

The State Secret

Sericulture is the name given to the different processes in the cultivation of silk. The discovery of how to unwind silk from the cocoon and use the thread for weaving precious fabrics was of immense importance to the Emperor, so controls were put in place to ensure that the secret remained within the court. There is very little reliable documentation of this early period but the key to maintaining the secret was to keep each part of the process separate, so that no one knew the whole story.

The provinces around the Yanghzte Basin had the perfect climate for growing mulberry trees, the *morus alba*, the preferred food of the tiny indigenous silkworm, the *Bombyx mandarina Moore*. Sericulture was established there and the local people learnt to care for and cherish their silkworms. By royal decree, at the end of each season, the cocoons were collected, bundled up into large sacks and transported to another district. There the villagers looked forward to the arrival of the cocoons, and the work and income that they represented. They boiled the cocoons to free the silk fibre from the gummy sericin and reeled and tied the silk into skeins. Sometimes the thread was 'thrown', which twisted the fibres together to make them stronger and more resilient. These people knew about reeling,

Wicker trays of silkworms and mulberry leaves, tended by three ladies.
From T'ien-kung k'ai-wu, by Sung Ying-sing, 1637.

throwing and skeining silk, not of how the silk came to be on the cocoon. The skeins were packaged into fardels or bundles and once again sent vast distances to be dyed, or to major weaving centres like Sichuan. The very best silk was sent to the court itself.

Within the court was the gynaeceum, the women's weaving workshop, where highly skilled weavers wove the best silk into beautiful fabrics for the use of the Emperor and his court. One select group of women came from a long line of court weavers and commanded the highest esteem, because they alone knew the secret skills of weaving the cryptic and mysterious pattern known as the Sacred Eye. The knowledge of this particular technique had been jealously guarded and handed down from mother to daughter through many generations.

Handreeling the silk from the cocoons being soaked in the bowls of hot water. From T'ien-kung k'ai-wu, by Sung Ying-sing, 1637.

The people of each district only understood their particular aspect of sericulture. Hundreds of miles away, other villagers dealt with another part of the preparation of silk, so no one actually knew the whole story of how silk was made. There were heavy fines and penalties given to those who betrayed the secrets of silk, and great pressure was put on everyone associated with sericulture to ensure that the secrets were kept within the Middle Kingdom. In the villages and hamlets, gruesome folk-tales were told and retold, of spies caught trading the secrets of silk. There was also another method of punishment to ensure that no one spread the secrets. It was called decapitation.

The traditional date for the discovery of silk is 2640 BC, but China began cultivating and domesticating silk long before that. In one archaeological site, the outline of a silkworm, probably the tiny indigenous *Bombyx mandarina Moore*, was found carved into a little ivory cup, thought to be between 6000 and 7000 years old. Over the centuries, these primitive native silkworms were gradually superseded by the larger and more productive strain, the *Bombyx mori*. In 1927 on a neolithic site (7000-1500 BC) in Shanxi Province in Northern China, a *Bombyx mori* cocoon dated between 2600 and 1300 BC was found, deliberately cut in half, indicating that someone had actually handled it.

In recent years there have been some exciting discoveries of ancient textiles, like the little bundle of red silk ribbons and woven fragments, found at Qianshanyang in Zhejiang. They were carbon dated to around 3000 BC and seem to be one of the earliest actual examples of woven *Bombyx mori* silk. A bamboo basket containing scraps of woven silk was discovered in the ancient silk-growing district of Wu-hsing in Chekiang. Silk was used as wadding for winter garments and quilted bedding and one fragment of quilted silk taffeta has been dated to around 2800 BC. During the Shang Dynasty (c1600-1027 BC) silk wrapping cloths were used as part of burial rituals to wrap precious bronze and jade funereal items. The weave left an imprint or pseudomorph on the vessels as the silk decayed, and the ghost of the pattern can still be seen under special conditions.

Spindles and other spinning and weaving accessories have been found in sites along the lower Yangtzi River, but not looms or large pieces of equipment. Early looms were primitive affairs, with wooden cross members and a strap worn around the weaver's back. They were not large wooden structures like modern hand-looms, but simple pieces of wood and string and rather fragile. They could be rolled up and transported, but just as easily damaged and subject to decay, and so have not survived. All these discoveries help to confirm that sericulture was not only practiced in China from a very early date, but that the people had a sophisticated knowledge of the processes of unwinding the cocoons, throwing, dyeing, weaving, quilting and sewing.

The word for silk was incorporated into the written language, the characters sometimes woven into the silks. Jin, the Chinese word for brocade, was occasionally woven into the borders of some of the very early compound weave fabrics. Considering their early date

Korean backstrap loom, thought to be very similar to early Chinese looms. This izaribata loom has a single treadle and the shed is changed by dragging a cord attached to the weaver's foot.
From Cavendish, 'Korea and the Sacred White Mountain', 1894.

of around 1100 BC, these beautifully woven, multi-coloured, polychrome silks are technically most impressive. Silk quilts, gowns and burial cloths, also from around 300 BC, have been discovered in a Chu tomb in the Hubei Province. The workmanship is exquisite, the colours well-preserved and many have designs which feature flowers, swirling clouds and quaint stylized animals. Some of the decorative patterns are based on the shape of the silkworm or the cocoon. These early finds are the first glimmers of a developing silk industry.

Some of the earliest writing, in the form of pictograms on oracle bones, date from the Shang dynasty (1600 to 1027 BC). By 300 BC the actual words for silk, mulberry and silkworms are found inscribed on ancient shell and bronze articles. Silk paper is mentioned in early Chinese texts and examples have been found in a refuse site at Yamen near the Jade Gate, by the nineteenth century explorer Sir Marc Aurel Stein. These include a strip of white silk, written in Kharoshthi script which offers an early proof that silk was used for writing on, either before or in preference to paper. Among many other examples are two fragments of a letter from an officer named Zheng. He was stationed on the northern frontier and was writing to recommend a colleague to an officer garrisoned at Dunhuang.

Paper was initially made from rags and bark, but in 105 AD, Ts'ai Lun discovered that if short lengths of silk fibre were added during the pulp stage, they gave strength and durability to the paper. Between 100 BC and 300 AD, everyday information was written on cheap, wood or bamboo slips which were scraped clean and reused. To ensure security, these narrow slips were tied and sealed with a

Tomb Bricks from Xincheng, 20 km NW of Jiayuguan. A boy stands on guard to scare away predators while a man collects either mulberry leaves or silkworm cocoons from the tree. China Travel and Tourism Press.

layer of clay and stamped with the official's seal, or the clerk's 'chop'. Woven silk fabrics were preferred for the exquisite silk text rolls of the emperor's personal library. These sacred and literary texts found in graves in Central China, contain information on magic and mysticism and many are special presentation copies of maps, diagrams and treatise on astrology and medicine.

Gradually the knowledge and practice of sericulture spread throughout China; from Hainan in the south to Heilungkiang in the north, from Shantung in the east to Khotan in the west. Sericulture was established in Gansu province, where tomb bricks were painted with scenes of people picking mulberry leaves, silkworm breeding and silk weaving. The southern province of Chengdu, the ancient capital of Sichuan became so famous for its fine silk weaving that it was known as 'Brocade City'. The north-eastern provinces of Shantung and Lianoning became centres for the production of shantung and pongee silks. These wild silkworms require a temperate climate. Tussah silks have been produced there from the time of the Han and Wei dynasties.

Gifts, Tribute and Trade

Gorgeous, colourful, decorative and precious woven silks made desirable and prestigious tribute gifts. In Shu Ching's history of the Chinese philosopher Confucius, dated around 500 BC, the Chinese Emperor, the Great Yu (2205-2197 BC) demanded and got tribute gifts. The Book of Annuak specifically mentions lengths of blue and red silk as gifts from six provinces.

The word 'gift' is rather a misnomer. The Chinese system of gift and tribute was a subtle and highly sophisticated balance, reflecting both the quality and quantity of the gifts offered and the power and status of the people involved. The Emperor was believed to be the Son of Heaven, heir to the Middle Kingdom. All people were subordinate to him, bowed down and honoured him. On arrival, the visiting envoy made his offering of valuable gifts. The Emperor then gave orders for beautiful silks and other costly items to be assembled, though not quite as many or as valuable, to present to the envoy in exchange. The gifts were accepted with a great profusion of thanks and acknowledgement of obligation. The Emperor saw the gifts as a rightful tribute from a lesser to a greater power. To the envoy it was probably just trade by another name and so the balance of power was seen to be maintained. The envoy returned to his own country taking bolts of silk with him, but not the knowledge of sericulture. In this way, silk fabric, along with many other items, passed out of China.

In ancient times, the Chinese court rarely engaged in trade with other countries because it saw itself as superior and self-sufficient. Silk was the most unique and highly desired of any product, the envy of every other nation. It was not however, looked on as a source of income for the treasury because it was much simpler to just threaten the people and demand that they pay higher taxes. The court controlled the production and collection of silk so it was used as a gift to reward people. Like any commodity, it varied enormously in quality, colour, texture and the complexity of the weave. Each bolt of fabric was carefully graded and then allocated, following a set scale, to the person of the appropriate rank in the hierarchy. It was even used as a negotiable currency and state servants, officials and soldiers could be paid in cash or lengths of silk. One officer serving on the North West Frontier was given two rolls of silk to the value of 900 coins as his month's pay. Eventually silk turned up in the marketplace as an item of trade or exchange. By the time of the Han Dynasty (206 BC-220 AD), lengths of silk cloth, bags of cocoons or bundles of silk floss could replace money.

Sericulture was so widely practiced that silk became one of the recognized products used to fulfill one's tax obligations. In the seventh century AD, Yo was a handcraft or local product tax of 3%, which every able-bodied male between the ages of 22 and 60 was required to pay. Zoyo or corvée labour was another form of tax, requiring each male to work for ten days each year on a government project like road building. To avoid being conscripted, the farmer could offer 26 feet or 7.9 metres of cloth, silk floss or another local product in lieu of his labour. Cho was also a local tax paid to the Imperial Court, initially levied on each household. Eventually everyone was required to pay it in the form of rough silk, thread, silk floss, cloth, iron or salt. The only people exempt were those on military service. Each family had the responsibility to transport these products to the capital, and to pay for food and

Picking leaves from mulberry trees.
Copyright Bibliotheque Nationale, Paris.

accommodation while they were there. It was an enormous burden on the peasants and they complained and resorted to every subterfuge to evade these taxes. By the tenth century, the central authority was breaking down and these taxes were often surreptitiously diverted into the coffers of the tax collectors and powerful officials.

Silk spreads from China

No secret can be kept forever and with wars, trade and the passage of missionaries and adventurers, the secrets of silk gradually made their way east to Korea and Japan and northwest across the Eurasian Steppes to Russia, and south into India. Some of the oldest written references to Indian woven silk are in the sacred epics and Sanskrit texts, in the Ramayana and the Mahabharata. India had its own indigenous wild tussah silk moths, but the cultivation of a domestic variety of white silk was in the future.

Exciting stories abound of how the knowledge of sericulture spread around the world, stories rich in wars, espionage and mayhem. Sometime before 200 BC, Chinese silkworkers went to Korea, possibly not voluntarily as emigrants, but as slaves captured in war and made to work. There is evidence that during the early Mahan period in Korea, the Puyo people were wearing patterned silk clothes. Silk fabrics, dated from 28 BC, have been found in Japan, but the knowledge of sericulture took longer to spread throughout the islands. Japanese chronicles tell of how a Chinese prince and his household were exiled, possibly for some misdemeanor, and sought asylum in Japan, taking a real risk by bringing silkworm eggs with them as a gift. According to the Nihon Shoki chronicle, the Japanese government encouraged sericulture and collected silk as taxes as early as the fifth century AD. A temple was erected in the province of Sethu to these pioneer silk weavers, and the industry grew into one of national importance.

There are a number of different versions of one of the best loved stories of how silk reached Khotan on the furthest borders of Western China. A Tibetan legend of around 400 AD described how, as a token of his fidelity and veneration, the King of Khotan, sometimes known as Vijaya Jaya, petitioned the Chinese Emperor for the hand of a princess of the royal house. In her grief at leaving her family and going so far away without even the comfort of silk gowns and quilts, she decided to take a terrible risk and take both mulberry seeds and silkworm eggs hidden in her headdress. At the border, the guards searched the whole caravan, but Princess Punyesvara was not searched; she passed through the gates into Khotan and the knowledge of sericulture reached the far western territories. This version of the legend says she did not tell the King she had brought the silkworm eggs with her so when they hatched, the King's ministers accused her of breeding 'little poisonous snakes' and demanded that they be burnt. She was distraught at the thought of losing them after all the risks she had taken, but she managed to save a few and after they had spun their cocoons she showed the silk to the King. He quickly understood the importance of silk to her, and the priceless value to his kingdom of establishing sericulture.

A similar story was told in the history of the T'ang, the Tangshu, by the travelling Buddhist monk Hsuan Tsang (602-664 AD). China had only recently been re-unified under the T'ang dynasty and the King of Khotan heard rumours that silk existed in the east. He coveted this precious textile and sent a delegation to the Emperor T'ai-tsung to ask for a bride from the emperor's family and this was granted. The King's second request for silkworm eggs was forcibly denied and the Emperor had the border stations closely watched. Princess Wen-ch'eng decided to risk severe punishment by hiding the silkworm eggs in her clothing when she passed out of China and into Khotan. To celebrate her first successful batch of cocoons, she had an inscription carved in stone which said: 'It is prohibited to kill the silkworm. Only when the moth has left the cocoon may the silk be used.' In this version, silk could not be unreeled from the whole cocoon because the moth had made a hole through which to escape which broke the silk filament. This suggests that the silk fibre was spun in short lengths rather than reeled as a continuous thread.

Khotan flourished during the T'ang dynasty, but it is hard to tell from the stories the real extent of silk production. During excavations in 1914 in the desert near Dandan-Oilik, Sir Marc Aurel Stein found an ancient painting of a princess with a basket on her head of what look like cocoons. Nearby a girl is pictured weaving, while another girl points to the princess's hair. This may illustrate the legend and it helps to confirm that the knowledge of sericulture had already spread to Khotan.

Marc Aurel Stein identified the picture of the girl in the tomb painting as the Princess of Khotan, as she seems to have cocoons hidden in her headdress.

The Spread of Silk to the West

Although it was still not known exactly how silk was made, there are many references to silk in classical literature and wonderful misunderstandings and theories as to its origin. Aristotle (384-322 BC) mentions silk in his writings in 'Hist. anim,' V19 (17) 11. He describes the silkworm as a 'curious horned worm'. He credits a Phoenician princess, Pamphile, daughter of Plateus, on the island of Cos off the coast of Turkey, with the discovery of silk and describes the fabric she wove as 'woven wind'. The island of Cos produced an inferior wild silk, but Aristotle obviously valued it. The Roman historian Pliny (23-79 AD) agreed with him, and was convinced that silk grew on trees, saying in his Natural History (IV.54) that '...the Seres are famous for the wool from their forests. They remove the down from the leaves with the help of water', so he got it partly right, but clearly had not had first hand experience of sericulture. Virgil (70-19 BC) also describes how '... the Chinese comb off leaves their delicate down...' Flax and cotton are both vegetable fibres and were widely known in classical times, so Pliny and Virgil probably expected silk to come from a similar source.

The Bible also has at least three references to silk. In the book of Ezekiel, written around 300 BC, in Chapter 16, verse 10, it says 'I clothed thee also in broidered work and shod thee with badger's skin and girded thee about with fine linen and covered thee with silk,' and in verse 13: 'Thus wast thou decked with gold and silver and thy raiment too was of fine linen and silk and broidered work.' In the Book of Proverbs it says, ' She maketh herself coverings of tapestry: her clothing is silk and purple.' Even in biblical times, silk was known and valued and considered most precious.

There is also a Babylonian legend told by Ovid (43 BC-17 AD) in his *Metamorphosis*. It is a real Romeo and Juliet story, the one Shakespeare retells as a comic piece in his *Midsummer Night's Dream*. Ovid's story tells how Pyramus and Thisbe, when their parents refused to allow them to marry, arranged to meet secretly under a mulberry tree. Disaster struck when Thisbe, who arrived first, was frightened by a lion that grabbed her scarf. The lion had recently killed an ox and when Pyramus found the scarf covered in blood but no Thisbe, he believed that the lion had attacked and killed her and he killed himself. Thisbe found Pyramus dead and killed herself which is why, legend says, the white mulberry tree has black fruit, which drips blood red juice. These imaginative stories certainly added to the romance and mystery of silk.

Beautiful silk textiles gradually became more readily available in Central Asia and Persia. The Persians quickly established themselves as the sole middlemen between East and West, but then war broke out between Byzantium and Persia, and the west was cut off from its supply of silk. In Byzantium, Emperor Justinian I (c482-565 AD) had his capital and power base at Constantinople. He was one of the most brilliant and ablest of leaders, but he had become increasingly anxious as his prosperous and pleasure-loving people squandered their money on luxuries and in particular on gorgeous imported silks. Two-thirds of the Byzantine Empire's treasury went on imports of luxury items from the East. High court and church dignitaries dressed lavishly in silk, emblazoned with imperial purple insignia. The wealthy people paraded in the finest silk robes and were buried in silk winding sheets.

Justinian at the moment when the two Nestorian monks hand him the hollow cane containing the silkworm eggs.

14

Justinian had a real problem keeping his people focused on the priorities. There was a cavalier attitude to the necessity of holding a treasure chest and being prepared for the serious business of war. If silk could be produced locally, then trade would no longer have to go through Persia and the other nations that demanded exorbitant bribes and taxes. Further, the quantity and price of this luxury item could be controlled by the Byzantine state. The collection of a local tax on silk would not go amiss, either. A little international espionage was called for, as the knowledge of sericulture was still a closely guarded secret denied to the west.

Two travelling Nestorian monks saw an opportunity and obtained an audience with Justinian and convinced him that they could bring him the secrets of silk. There is some doubt as to whether the monks went to China or Northern India to get the silkworm eggs. Procopius of Caesarea, who died in 562 AD, said that the monks had spent time in a country called Serinda, an early name for China, where the silkworm eggs were covered with dung, to keep them warm. (War of the Goths, IV, 17). The sixth century Roman chronicler Theophanes maintained they went to India and the journey to get the silkworm eggs took two years. On their return in 552 AD the two dusty, travel-worn monks were taken into Justinian's presence. They bowed deeply and then up-ended their hollow cane walking sticks. Out tumbled mulberry seeds and tightly rolled twists of paper with the tiny silkworm eggs attached. The eggs had been kept cool during the journey, waiting for the warmth of spring when they would hatch out. The monks were suitably rewarded and given every assistance to get sericulture established. Imperial workshops were set up by the church and state to try to monopolize and control production. These were also known as gynaeceum, but they were staffed by both men and women. Despite royal backing, the quantities of silk required by the citizens of Byzantium were far more than the new industry could support and silk still had to be imported. But, as in China, no secret can be kept forever. The knowledge of sericulture was dispersed, and the European silk industry developed from these beginnings.

The Silk Road through the high mountains in northern Pakistan. The harsh conditions are obvious in the narrow tracks high on the barren scree and rock slopes above the Indus River.

Chapter 2
The Silk Road, From East to West

Central Asia has always been a challenge to those who tried to cross it. It extends for over 5000 miles, from the Black Sea via the Hindu Kush and the High Pamirs, across the vast Taklamakan and the Gobi deserts. Much of it is wasteland, harsh and inhospitable. It has deep craters and waterless ancient riverbeds and is partly ringed by soaring snow-covered mountains. Very occasionally it is temperate and gentle, a glimpse of heaven. From time immemorial, people have tried to control and conquer this ancient land. Whole nations have swept in, fighting, pillaging and claiming their right to be there and possess. Others have sought new pastures for their herds and new markets for their goods. Gradually over the last 5000 years, a cobweb of shifting trails to summer grazing lands, strings of watering holes and passes through high mountains have been established.

These tracks serviced traders and bandits, soldiers and government officials, tough resilient men able to withstand the violent, extreme changes in climate and terrain and to protect themselves and their goods. Over the centuries Buddhists,

Manichaeans, Zoroastrians, Confucians, Taoists, Muslims, Jews and Christians have journeyed thousands of miles to seek enlightenment and proclaim their message. Even more effective at spreading ideas than the official missionaries were the unofficial ones, the traders along the roads. The routes were a conduit for new ideas, new technology, new agricultural methods and sericulture. The Silk Route is the collective name for some of these patterns of travel, not one road, but a network of shifting tracks. It had no name at all until Baron Ferdinand von Richthofen (1833-1905), the German geographer and traveller, wrote his major work on China, *Aufgaben der Geographie* (1883). There he coined the phrase, *die Seidenstrassen,* the Silk Road.

Caravanserai, offering accommodation and shelter for the men and stabling for their animals, grew up around wells and at crossroads. There the men rested, replenished their supplies, acquired fresh pack animals, hired guides and traded their silk. Markets evolved, selling jewels, spices, medicines and slaves, any commodity that would turn a profit. The men travelled in groups for security, transporting the goods from one oasis or trading centre to another and then trading on. The High Pamirs formed a natural barrier so it was rare for Chinese merchants to go as far as Rome, or Romans to Ch'ang-an.

For a time, some routes would be favoured, the travellers welcomed, engaged in trade and helped on their way. Then the political regime changed and as cities were razed to the ground and

Caravanserai, where a camel waits patiently at the abandoned desert city of Gaochang.

lands conquered, new rulers imposed their wills. A harsh or greedy administration made the route too difficult, the bribes and taxes too high, the defenses too strong, so a new way had to be found. Changes in weather patterns and terrain stopped people from crossing boundaries. The violent, whirling sand storm known as the kara buran, buried whole cities. Oases dried up and the salt flats took over where once there had been vegetation and fresh water to feed the travellers and their animals.

Trade along the Silk Road

All the various prerequisites of trade were set up along the silk routes including mints to produce a dependable and valid coinage. The Macedonian merchant Maes Titianus produced a travellers' guide. He did not travel, but his agents returned with information about the actual routes, services and conditions and colourful stories about Sera Metropolis, the City of Silk, probably Ch'ang-an, and Sinae Metropolis, possibly Loyang. Letters survive from traders from the second century BC. They had to be cleared through a merchants' organization called the Karum and often state 'you are my brother' or 'you are my father', indicating that the person was an agent trading on their behalf, aware of their requirements and preferences. Wherever there were men with a sense of adventure and purpose, a lust for life and riches, there you would find silk. Silk was a high profit item, relatively easy to transport and always in high demand. Providing the taxes and bribes were paid, the goods got through, despite governments, wars or lack of a common language.

The usual language of trade was Aramaic, especially in the lowlands. The 'koine' or common language gradually replaced Aramaic, while in the highlands, Persian was the norm. Trade was not necessarily conducted in an organized manner. Some people used a secret, 'silent trade' system, later described in the first century AD by Pomponius Mela in his '*Chorography*'. At an agreed site, goods were displayed and the trader left so that another could lay his goods for exchange, beside them. There was much adding and subtracting of items until a balance was achieved. Then each trader came and claimed his exchanged goods and departed, often without actually meeting or speaking a word. Sometimes it was not the lack of language but the need for secrecy that led to another form of 'silent trade'. Here the traders would meet and clasp each other's hand within their wide sleeves. The traders' inscrutable, weathered faces gave nothing away as they tapped out the prices and conditions on each other's palm until a deal was agreed. The transaction terms were arranged and finalized without curious onlookers ever discovering the details.

By the second century BC, the Kushan Empire had conquered Bactria which lay at the meeting point of the great trading routes: the road south to India, the Silk Road linking China with Parthian Iran and Roman Syria, and the road to the Black Sea which went north of the Caspian Sea and the Caucasus Mountains. The Parthians on the wide Iranian Plateau established their vast territory straddling the Silk Road, and very quickly realized that great profits could be made by controlling the Western section of the route and demanding the payment of taxes and bribes. The Chinese too, soon set up commercial and political links, and a Chinese chronicle dated 106 BC recorded what was believed to be the first major caravan from China to An-hsi, Parthia, and the Iranian Plateau. By 60 BC the Chinese controlled both the southern and northern routes of the Eastern sector of the Silk Road. The trader Pam Ch'iao wrote to his brother Pan Ku, saying ' I now send 300 pieces of white silk which I want you to trade for Bactrian horses, some rugs and (the aromatic) storax '. The domination by the two Empires, the Han in the East and the Persian to the West, helped to ensure peace and security on the route and trade flourished.

By now China had developed a practical foreign policy and was in effect happy to trade. However, it still retained the fictions of

The Great Wall of China is usually made of local materials and here at Jiayuguan its is made of layers of reeds and hard compacted loess from the surrounding Gobi desert.

'tribute' and 'gifts', which fitted its vision of itself as a civilizing society and the Confucian ideal of order and Imperial Virtue. Large quantities of silk were increasingly used in exchange for tribute, to enforce control and compliance from neighbouring states. It was also used to pay soldiers' wages and for other services, so some silk was traded on. This policy, largely based on silk, did stimulate commercial activity, but was financially ruinous to the Han economy. The annals carefully record all gifts and exchanges. In 51 BC China gave Huhanxie, a suzerain from one of the neighbouring territories, 77 sets of bedcovers and two years later the same again, plus 110 sets of clothing. Later records mention other gifts totalling 8000 pieces of embroidered silk and 6000 pounds of silk floss. Fifty years later, these gifts had expanded to 84,000 pieces of embroidered silk and 78,000 pounds of silk floss. Yu Ying-shih calculated that the system absorbed seven per cent of the total revenue of the Empire, excluding military and administrative expenses. Naturally, some men tried to take advantage of the system and made false claims. In 166 AD a merchant arrived in Tonkin from Rome saying he was an emissary from the Roman Emperor Marcus Aurelius Antoninius, but he was found out and discredited.

It became an extensive two-way traffic. It was estimated that there were at least twelve great caravans a year of camels, men and goods. Furs came from Russia, ivory from India and jade from Central Asia, which was especially highly valued by the Chinese. Pearls and gems flowed west to Antioch, Damascus and the coastal cities. China exported to the western regions vast quantities of silk, skeins of yarn and bolts of cloth, the finest coming from the Imperial Workshops. Exquisite Chinese fabrics from the Han and later T'ang

A Bactrian camel, with its fardels of silk as depicted in Matthew Paris' map of the Holy Land in his Chronica majora.
With permission of the Master and Fellows of Corpus Christi College, Cambridge.

dynasties have been discovered in burial sites along these routes. The colours still glow and many feature embroideries using satin and knot stitches, quilting and fine applique work. The Chinese had a fascination with all things western so woollens, linens, coral, amber, lacquer and glass were transported overland to China. Glassmaking was first developed in Sidon around the first century BC and was highly valued as it was not manufactured in China until the fifth century AD. Cinnamon bark, spices and rhubarb, desired for their medicinal purposes, were traded along the route as were military items, bronze and iron, asbestos, mirror and ostriches which the Chinese called 'camel birds'. They believed all these wonderful items came from Da Qin, Great Rome, their name for the Roman Empire. The Romans simply called their territory *'orbis terrarum'* or 'The World'. It was still a very unequal trade; there was far more silk going west than other items going east.

Silk in the West

Territories are won and empires expanded through success in war, and trade follows. After Alexander the Great's death in 323 BC, Ptolemy I (c367-283 BC) claimed Egypt as his portion of the vast empire. The capital Alexandria soon became wealthy, and fairs and centres for artisans were established. Effectively, it was the western end of the spice route from India to Egypt. Silk fabrics have been found buried in the graves of some of the bandits who preyed on travellers along the route so it was clearly used for transporting silk to the Mediterranean. The opulent silks captured the imagination of the luxury loving Egyptians and they called China Serica, the Land of Silk. Cleopatra (69-30 BC), the last ruler of the Ptolemic line in Egypt, exploited the exotic and alluring qualities of silk and the ravishing, diaphanous silks she wore certainly made her ministers nervous and contributed to her reputation as a temptress.

The largest share of Alexander's former Empire was claimed, then governed by the first Seleucid, Seleucus Nicator (c358-280 BC). The area included Persia, Afghanistan, Bactria, Syria, Mesopotamia and Armenia. Seleucus knew that silk would bring prestige and wealth to his nation and that the control of it would increase his own power, so he tried to direct the silk trade towards the seaport of Antioch, one of the western focal points of the Silk Road. Later, the city gave its name to Antioch cloth, a type of figured silk brocade, patterned with birds, whose heads, beaks and feet were picked out in gold. Another equally important city, Seleucia, was built on the banks of the Tigris near the decaying city of Babel and it became the main Mesopotamian crossroad city for the silk trade.

There is something exotic and mysterious about silk, so it often features in fables and tales of battles and acts of daring and courage. The appearance of vibrantly coloured silk banners at the Battle of Carrhae near the Euphrates River in 53 BC influenced the outcome of an important battle and the course of history. The powerful, opposing Parthian archers, banners aloft, came thundering down towards the Roman legions led by Marcus Licinius Crassus, the Governor of Syria. The Romans had never seen such dazzling colours; they panicked, broke ranks and fled at the sight of the advancing cavalcade. The triumphant Parthians gloried in their success, yet within ten years and peace at last between the Romans and the Parthians, similar banners were flying all over Rome, this time in honour of Julius Caesar, back from one of his triumphant campaigns.

Silk was still scarce and expensive, but the Roman citizens wanted their share of the luxuries of life. The richest and most powerful Romans, at this time, wore only small pieces of silk, circles, strips or squares, sewn onto their toga and tunics. These silk fragments were the insignia of power, the mark of a patrician, especially when they were dyed purple or embroidered with gold or silver thread. Gradually, fine silk fabrics became more readily available, but still at a price. Those people who saw themselves as leaders, politically, economically or socially, sought to display their wealth, taste and power by wearing the latest fashion. The Roman philosopher Seneca (5BC-65 AD) became gravely concerned at the display of sparkling, translucent silks. He wrote, 'I see silken clothes, if one can call them clothes at all, that in no degree afford protection either to the body or the modesty of the wearer, and clad in which no woman could honestly swear she is not naked.'

The Roman Emperor Tiberius (14-37 AD) around the same time as Seneca, also tried to shame his subjects from wearing silk, saying it 'confuse men with women' (Annals III 53). Tacitus in his Annals II 33 forbade men to 'disgrace themselves by wearing of silk materials', but in reality, it made no difference at all.

A legend credits Pamphile, the daughter of Plateus on the Island of Cos with the discovery of sericulture and how to weave silk. The artist illustrating this story from Boccaccio's In Praise of Famous Women, *unfortunately did not understand that it was the silkworm, not the cocoon that had legs and ate mulberry leaves.* Bibliotheque Nationale, Paris.

Pliny (23-79 AD) also became critical of the way '… a lady would appear in public in transparent dress'. He went on to say '…they unravel the heavy silk fabrics and re-weave them into shimmering gauzes, known as 'glass togas' and it is through such difficult work that our women form the double task of separating the strands and reweaving them'. Pliny had only a limited understanding of sericulture and weaving, as he still thought silk grew on trees, so he probably did not fully understand just how difficult it would be to unravel silk fabrics, split the thicker threads into finer ones and reweave them. Loosely woven, poor quality fabric will fray, and the fine threads often break and become tangled and useless for reweaving, though short broken threads can be incorporated in tapestry weaving. Silk fibre was imported into Rome in both skeins and bundles, as well as bolts of cloth, and could have been woven locally, to the current requirements of the fashion conscious citizens. Light-weight plain weave fabric is relatively simple to produce, but the exotic, richly patterned silks would still have been imported at vast expense.

Men continued to deck themselves out in the most brilliant silks, many squandering a fortune, to the extent that the Roman Emperor Vesparian (69-79 AD) became extremely worried by the enormous quantities of precious silks being imported and the consequent outpouring of gold bullion from the treasury. Pliny maintained that 100 million Roman sesterces were transferred each year in trade with India, Seres and Arabia, much for the purchase of silk.

In the West there was still no clear idea about the origin of silk and many educated men tried to offer an explanation. In the second century AD, the Greek geographer and historian Pausanias no longer accepted Pliny's statement that silk was plant-based and that 'The first men who were involved in it were the Seres, famous for the wool of their forests.' Pausanius would have been aware of the legends of Pamphile, the goddess who was said to have discovered silk on the Greek island of Cos, but he was not at all clear on every point. In his 'Description of Greece' (VI, 26), he maintains that silk came from a little animal that the Greeks called 'Ser'. The rest is fantasy because he described the animal as being twice the size of a scarab and resembling the spiders that made their webs in the trees. He described how these silk spiders had eight legs around which they wrapped the fine thread. They lived in cages and the Seres fed them millet seed for the first four years and then during the fifth year, gave them a green reed to eat until they burst. He then stated categorically that the best silk was inside the corpse where the greater part of the thread was found. It was an imaginative explanation, but as he was an educated and widely travelled man, and there was already wild silk in Greece, it was all rather farfetched.

A Time of Change

With drought conditions increasing during the early years of the first century AD, the nomadic people of the Asian Steppes were on the move seeking better pastures for their herds. They struck terror in the hearts of the vulnerable villagers by their strength and number, as they ranged across the land. The Roman, Bactrian and Chinese Empires were beginning to decline, yet the Parthians continued to prosper because the most viable route was through their territory. From the time of Augustus Caesar (63 BC-14 AD) the main routes across Central Asia had been relatively safe and well organized, but financially punitive because of the bribes and taxes demanded en route.

As a result, both East and West looked to expand their seaborne foreign trade. It was organized into several stages using a combination of sea and land routes, depending on the season and weather, and the likelihood of being attacked by pirates. Persian ships would go to Canton in China then back via Malaya and India, buying silks and spices. Some Chinese silk went overland to Alexandria and the Phoenician cities, now in present day Lebanon, to be dyed and woven before being shipped on to Rome and other ports in Europe. By this time the monsoon was known to Indian and Arab sailors, but not in the West, so it was not until 50 AD that a Greek captain from Egypt started using the monsoon winds to sail directly from the Red Sea ports to India. Navigation was still difficult so sailors followed the coastline by day and took their bearings from the stars by night. As knowledge of the seas increased, Romans began to transport men and merchandise by sea, thus avoiding the Parthians altogether.

In Rome, the trade in silk continued to flourish despite official disapproval and by 380 AD, a Roman historian noted peevishly that silk 'once confined to the nobility, now spread to all classes without distinction, even to the lowest'. The wearing of silk was a way of indicating a person's status within society, an outward and visible sign of wealth, power and refinement, and without these distinctions it was hard to tell who was important. Some of the most luxurious silk was worth its weight, ounce for ounce in gold, its cost having increased by up to forty times. These imported silks were exquisitely woven, with complex patterns, embroidered and encrusted with jewels and dyed using the most costly means. All manner of people, aristocrats, clerics and merchants, as well as fashionable women, were abandoning their simpler styles and wearing sophisticated silk clothes. Silk had taken Rome by storm.

Rome still had to pay for its silk in gold, with serious consequences for the economy. Rome had been in gradual decline since around 200 AD and the financial impact on the treasury of importing vast quantities of silk was a significant contributor to Rome's downfall. Gold was pouring from the treasury to pay for the luxuries demanded by its citizens. When the Visigoths (376-410) had Rome under siege, their leader Almaric demanded and got from the city a ransom which included 5000 pounds of gold, 30,000 pounds of silver and 4000 silk tunics.

The Persians continued to control silk crossing the Iranian Plateau. Rome was the major silk supplier to Western Europe so to their mutual benefit, they negotiated a commercial agreement naming the Persian silk city of Nisibus in Iranian Mesopotamia as the official centre for purchasing silk for the West. Christianity was spreading and one branch, the Nestorians, set up a theological college in Nisibus. Constantine's (274-337 AD) conversion to what became Orthodox Christianity, gave the religion official status in the Byzantine Empire. Prodigious quantities of luxurious silks were required and the churches shimmered and glowed with silken hangings, heavily embroidered with gold and silver. Silk was used for liturgical vestments for the clergy and winding cloths for the dead. Within a short space of time there were five guilds in his capital city Constantinople, trading or working exclusively in silk to supply the church, state and populous.

The silk road was changing. The Indian traders took the southwest routes via the Karakorum and Kashmir passes into India. The Sogdians continued to trade north through western Turkestan to the Eurasian Steppe. Sericulture had already spread to Merv, and was especially successful around the Caspian Plain. Then a Persian raiding party abducted some Syrian silk weavers and dyers and

Fragment of a very fine 9th century Byzantine silk known as the Earth and Ocean silk, probably made in Constantinople and now in the Treasury of Durham Cathedral. The roundels contain fish and swimming ducks representing the ocean, while the borders display grapes and other fruits. By permission of the Dean and Chapter of Durham Cathedral.

imprisoned them in their gynaeceum, forcing them to weave silk destined for the Eastern Roman Empire. With the help of the Syrian silkworkers, the Persians mastered the art of silk weaving and developed unique patterns and techniques. It was a long time, however, before they could produce sufficient silk for their own use, let alone excess to trade.

There were intermittent wars between the Persians and Romans and sometimes supplies were cut off altogether. Both the Syrian Desert route and the road to the weaving and dyeing cities of Phoenicia were threatened with bandits and charged high taxes. Constantinople's ruler Emperor Justinian I (c482-565) actively campaigned to restore the Empire to its ancient limits, reuniting the East and West. He and his stunning wife Theodora (c500-547) were intelligent, ambitious, courageous and very able administrators. She was the daughter of Aracius, a bear-feeder in the amphitheatre at Constaninople, and had been what is euphemistically described as an actress and dancer. Theodora, as Justinian's powerful and trusted helpmate, frequently bore responsibility for government at home, while he was absent on campaigns. She was generous with her wealth and had a particular interest in the welfare of women, especially those on the streets. Both rulers loved luxury and surrounded themselves with every conceivable extravagance, but were very astute to the needs of both the government and the people. To this day they can be seen in all their finery, in the mosaic frieze in the Church of San Vitale in Ravenna. Theodora always wore the richest silk, splendidly embroidered with stylized flowers and geometric patterns, typical of Byzantium. She stands regally, wearing a white undergown and maniakis embroidered with precious stones and interwoven with gold, and over that a purple palla or mantle embroidered with figures of the Magi. Around her neck she wears a very distinctive gold collar and on her head a heavy diadem with cascades of emeralds and pearls.

With the help of two Nestorian monks, Justinian had established sericulture near Constantinople. Procopius (499-565) his Prefect, was alone in criticizing Theodora. He maintained that she put the whole matter of silk production in the hands of one of her favourites, who created a royal monopoly, secretly enriching himself at the same time. As Theodora died in 547, before the arrival of the monks, perhaps Procopius was inventing slanderous stories for his own end. Justinian tried to control the production of silk by charging

Empress Theodora, the beautiful and capable wife of Justinian, wearing a rich and colourful silk tunic with woven or embroidered borders, a decorated maniakis embossed with jewels, and a diadem, called a stephanos with cascading pearls and gems.

nine chrysos a pound, too expensive for the Persian merchants. It was a time of great unrest and the silk industry collapsed leaving the silk weavers and craftsmen destitute, and many fled to the silk workshops of Persia.

The Islamic religion spread to Turkey, across to North Africa and on to Spain and with it went the silk trade, knowledge of sericulture and weaving the beautiful arabesque brocades. Mohammed was a trader and camel driver and Islam encouraged traders and accorded them high social status. The Byzantine Christians and the Moslems had generally cooperated and traded together, until Pope Urban II, in response to the advance on the Levant by the Saracens, announced the call to the Crusades at the end of the 11th century. In 1146 Roger II, King of Sicily, conducted raids on Thebes, Athens and Corinth. Greece had its own silk industry, built around the wild tussah varieties of silkworm, not the domesticated Bombyx mori. Nevertheless when Roger II deported silk weavers and embroiderers to Palermo, they were a real prize. The King set the silkworkers up in workshops and they helped to establish sericulture and silk weaving and taught the local people. It was another century before sericulture passed from Sicily to Lucca, Venice and Florence in Italy. By 1258 Venice was receiving silk muslins and brocades from Baghdad, Yezd, Malabar and China.

A Chinese war vessel with both sails and oars, with archers and men on the look out for pirates.

In the late 1300s Samarkand was still a vibrant city, a staging post for vast caravans of over 800 camels bringing fine silks from China and luxury items from the west. People still travelled the Silk Road, with the silk traders travelling all year, and the Islamic pilgrims mainly during the month of Ramadan. The Muslim world became united by cultural ties and trade, though less so politically. The spread of Islam effectively cut off Europe from Asia. China under the Ming Dynasty (1366-1644) withdrew and closed its western frontiers, and by the time Constantinople fell in 1453 to the Ottoman Turks, the great days of the Silk Road were over. It is no longer easy to travel the whole length from Ch'ang-an to the Mediterranean. It was virtually abandoned soon after Marco Polo's seventeen years in the Court of Kublai Khan. In remote and ruined desert cities, shards of Chinese pottery and vestiges of ancient silk patterns and designs can still be found, an echo of days long gone.

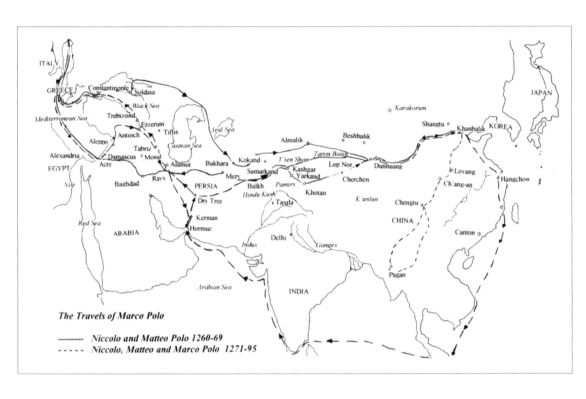

The Travels of Marco Polo

——— Niccolo and Matteo Polo 1260-69
- - - - - Niccolo, Matteo and Marco Polo 1271-95

Chapter 3
Marco Polo and his Discoveries of Silk along the Old Silk Road

The Saracens were on the march. The Europeans were afraid that the Saracen infidels or unbelievers would conquer and claim the Holy Land and impose their Muslim faith, so on the 27th November 1095, Pope Urban II announced the First Crusade. Christians rallied to the call to join the Holy Army and in the wake of successive Crusades, the route from Europe to the East was opened up. The Italian Mediterranean trading cities of Venice, Genoa and Pisa prospered and expanded. In 1204 Venice attacked and took Constantinople, enabling many wealthy Venetian merchants to set up trading posts in the Crimea and around the Black Sea. Venice became the richest and most powerful of the city states and a major sea power. The Venetian merchants won both ways, handling and trading goods coming from the East and supplying the army going to the Crusades with transport and provisions. They were ruthless bargainers and later claimed a half share of all Eastern conquests. The situation was ripe for political and mercantile expansion.

Around the same time, the Tartars of Mongolia, led by the great Genghis Khan (1162-1227), were hell-bent on conquering the whole known world, including the ancient Chinese Empire. When the Khan died, power passed to his third son, Ogadai, who reigned until 1241. He was followed by his son Kuyuk and eventually Kublai Khan (1252-1294), a man of great energy, vision and talent, who now controlled most of Central Asia.

The Tartars over-ran the whole of southern Russia, decimated Persia and advanced towards the West, pillaging and subjugating the towns and people as they went. This made many of the rulers of the lands around the Mediterranean extremely anxious. They began to fear the Tartars, the Saracens, and for the survival of the Christian Church. This motivated Pope Alexander IV in 1260 to publish his Papal Bull, *Clamat in auribus,* deploring the situation, warning every Christian ruler of the dire state of affairs and calling on the Church and people to respond.

A previous Pope, Innocent IV, had tried to defuse the situation and turn the Tartars away from their destructive path, and even better, to convert them to the True Christian Faith. In April 1245 he had sent a very fat, elderly, Italian friar, Giovanni di Piano Carpini (c1182-c1253) as an ambassador to Batu Khan. Carpini had very little understanding of the ways of the East, but his 'Voyages', written in 1246, did give a detailed account of Mongol life and laws, costume and society. He recorded the enthronement of Kuyuk, grandson of Genghis Khan, and described how Kuyuk stood under a double canopy of embroidered silk baldakin cloth of gold, while over 4000 ambassadors stood for hours, waiting in the crowd to offer gifts and tribute. These gifts included 500 carts, full of silver and gold and silken garments, all to be divided later among the Khan's court. Carpini described the rich 'robes of samit and robes of purple and baldakin cloth, silke girdles wrought with gold, costly skines and other gifts'. Carpini and his mission was of minor concern to the Khan and does not seem to have had the slightest effect on him or stopped the advance of his troops on the West.

In 1253 the saintly Louis IX of France sent a French Fleming, Friar William of Rubruk on a religious mission to Karakorum. William was not quite so large or so old as Carpini and had a much greater understanding of the people and their languages. He was the first European to realize that Cathay was actually China, the home of the silk traders '...from whom are bought the most excellent stuffes of silk'. In his 'Journal' he also described the women's garments as being similar to the men's but longer, worn with strange side opening jackets. He was no more effective than Carpini in converting the Khan to Christianity or stopping him advancing on the West.

The Polo Brothers

Marco Polo's adventure came at a critical time in history. The *Travels of Marco Polo* offers an insight into an exciting period of high adventure and exploration on the Old Silk Road. His book was unique in providing a wonderful record of just how extensive sericulture and silk products were in Mongol China.

Marco Polo's father and uncle, Niccolo and Matteo Polo were European merchants, not missionaries. They had their own ships, and traded in a wide variety of merchandise, specializing in gems which had a high value and were easy to carry, hide and trade. Versions of the story differ, but sometime before 1260, when Marco was still a young child, the Polo brothers left their families in Venice to visit their elder brother Marco senior, who had set up a trading post in Soldaia, now called Sudak, on the coast of the Crimea. Later they went on to Sarai, northwest of Astrakhan on the Caspian Sea where Barka Khan welcomed them, accepted their goods, and traded them '...for at least twice their value...' which was most satisfactory.

The Polo brothers stayed twelve months, but as the way back was blocked by a bitter local war, they headed eastwards towards the steppes and the Golden Horde looking to trade in Russia. They crossed the Volga and travelled to Bukhara, where they stayed at the court of Khan Hagatai. Once again the way back was blocked by regional wars and skirmishes, so after three years they took the opportunity to accompany an emissary of Kublai Khan to Khanbalik, near modern Beijing.

In 1265 Kublai Khan had been supreme ruler for about five years. He was a hard and powerful man, but among his many endearing qualities was his avid curiosity. He welcomed the Polo brothers warmly, entertained them with feasts and plied them endlessly with questions about life, religions and customs in the West, especially miracles, magical signs and portents.

The Polo brothers took the opportunity to trade their gems and become more fluent in the languages of the Far East. After a year Kublai Khan reluctantly let them go, on condition that they return to Khanbalik with holy oil from the sepulchre at Jerusalem and one hundred learned doctors of the church. He wanted educated, intelligent men, articulate in theology who could argue the case for Christianity.

The brothers left in the spring of 1266 with the Khan's blessing, supplies for the long journey and a golden tablet to

Messer Marco Polo, a fashionable young man. From the first German edition of his Travels, printed in Nuremberg in 1477, illustration reproduced in Henry Yule's Book of Ser Marco Polo, *1874.*

Early woodcut of Venetian traders being transported by boat

Kublai Khan handing Niccolo and Matteo Polo a golden table to ensure their safe journey and access to goods and services on their way back to Venice in 1266.
From Le Livre des Merveilles du Monde, reprinted in Henry Yule's Book of Ser Marco Polo *1874.*

ensure their protection and safe passage. They retraced their route to Bukhara and then headed straight to the Mediterranean via Baghdad before heading south to Acre, in Palestine, arriving there in April 1269. It had taken over three years to get back because of the appalling conditions, scorching deserts, terrible storms, treacherous snow-covered mountain ranges and swollen rivers.

In Acre they told Tebaldo Visconti (Tebaldo di Piacenza), the Papal Legate for Jerusalem, of their travels and the Khan's request. Tebaldo was most interested in the expansion of Christianity, but he felt unable to authorize one hundred learned men because the main universities could not supply that many scholarly men at any one time, and anyway, that decision would have to come directly from the Pope. Unfortunately there wasn't a Pope either. Pope Clement IV had died in 1268 and, with no news of the election of a new Pope, the brothers decided to return to Venice to see their families and attend to their businesses.

The Polo brothers had been away from Venice for nearly ten years, and they were greeted on their return with the sad news that Niccolo's wife had died. The little son he had left behind was now a lively, intelligent and observant young man. In Venice in 1268, there was a colourful and impressive procession of the guilds before the Palace of St Mark, to celebrate the institution of the new Doge, Lorenzo Tiepolo. Martino da Canale described the 50 sailing ships and galleys sailing past in the harbour and the guildsmen marching

in their ranks, wearing their dazzling livery. There were furriers wearing samite and scarlet silk, mantles of ermine and vair, the mercers in silk and the weavers of cloth of gold and all their servants dressed in rich purple shot silk. The luxurious silks must have left a strong impression because Marco's book is full of descriptions of wonderful clothes and textiles, especially the silks. He was completely enchanted by all he saw and by the tales his father and uncle told of their journey, and was determined not to be left behind again.

A new Pope still had not been elected. In exasperation the church officials locked the cardinals in conclave to await the puffs of smoke that proclaimed a successful election. In 1271 the three Polos felt they could wait no longer and decided to return to Acre. In Acre there was still no news of a new Pope so they decided to go to Jerusalem and get the holy oil. They got as far as Laiassus, a trading port for silks from the East, (1:1) north of Acre, when a messenger arrived in a great flurry and told them that a new Pope had at last been elected. He was none other than their old friend Tebaldo, now to be known as Pope Gregory X.

The three Polos leaving Venice with its bridges and canals and the Doges's Palace on the left.
From an English manuscript , c1400, Les Livres du Graunt Caam, MS Bodley 264, f218.
Bodleian Library, Oxford

The new Pope was still enthusiastic about christianising the Mongols, but had difficulty in arousing in his clergy a missionary zeal to travel to the far ends of the earth. They had enjoyed a fine lifestyle as part of the Papal Legate's court, were concerned about their careers and most reluctant to exchange the prestige and comfort there, for the dangers and discomforts of the unknown road and missionary life. Eventually two Dominicans, Friar Nicolo of Vicenza and Friar William of Tripoli, reluctantly accepted the mission to go to the Far East and convert the Mongols and the Chinese. The Pope invested them with wide powers and privileges, but within days, the two young men had become frightened by the scrapping between the Egyptians and the Armenians and

fearful for their lives. They thrust the Papal Papers and Privileges into the Polos' hands, and scurried back to Acre and the security of the Papal court. With a heavy heart the Polos decided to travel on, at all speed. They were very concerned that the Khan would not take kindly to both the delay and the lack of men to argue the case for Christianity.

Marco loved travelling and was obviously delighted with all he saw, especially the silks. He was very observant, but he tended to declare that all silks were the finest and richest, rather than note the differences. Nevertheless the book of his travels offers a unique picture of the breadth of sericulture and the beautiful silks produced in Mongol China at the time.

Marco made notes as they travelled. When they passed through Turkey, he saw that the Greeks and Armenians made a livelihood from trade and crafts, and he declared that the carpets of dyed crimson silks and other rich and delicate colours were the finest of all. (1:3) They travelled on to Turkomania, past Mt Ararat and Marco mentioned the oil field of Baku, on the inland Caspian Sea. He found evidence of Genoese traders who crossed the mountainous area of Ghelan and brought back the silk known by the same name (1:5), and was amazed by the abundance of 'silken fabrics and cloth of gold ... the finest ever seen', woven in Tiflis. (1.5) He was interested in different religions and races: Arabs who worshipped Mohammed, Nestorians, Jacobites and Christians. The Georgians, he noted, were Orthodox Christians and depended on trade for their livelihood. He mentioned the beautiful silk fabrics and cloth of gold, woven in the capital Tbilisi, and compared the silk and gold fabric called nasich, or nakh, with the brocades, damask and cramoisy or crimson cloth richly decorated with beasts and birds, made in Baldach (Baghdad).

The Polos continued their journey to the great commercial cities of Erzurum and Tabriz with their vast quantities of valuable cloth of gold brought in from India, Baghdad, and Mosul, including the material known as mosulin.(1.6) At that time it was woven from silk and gold thread and only later was made from cotton. Marco was less impressed by the large number of Latins and other traders whom he met there, who he thought were particularly wicked and treacherous.

In Baldach he described the manufacture of silk wrought with gold, and in particular the damasks and velvets ornamented with figures of birds and beasts, though this 'velluti' was probably carpet rather than velvet cloth. (1.7) He found silk and gold cloth traded at Tauris in Irak and in Yazd, (1.13) and a woven silk of the same name. It was in great demand by the merchants who made a good profit exporting it all over the known world. The Polos were heading for the city state of Kerman, via Saveh where the tomb of the Three Magi, Gaspar, Melchior and Baldasar was believed to be located. After that, it took seven more hard and unpleasant days to ride over the salt plains in the intense heat. They were attacked by some bandits, the Karaunas, (1.15) on the Kerman uplands and were lucky to escape with their lives. Once in Kerman they could relax and Marco was happy to watch the pretty girls there, embroidering birds and animals and other designs in multi-coloured silks on to curtains and bedcovers. (1.14)

They continued their travels south for another 200 miles to the Gulf of Hormuz, in the hope of getting a boat and making up for lost time, but the boats they were offered were flimsy and ramshackle, rough boards lashed together with loose twine and coconut husk and caulked with an extremely smelly fish glue, (1.17) so after much discussion they reluctantly abandoned their plan to go by ship, and retraced their steps to Kerman. There were 100 miles of desert to cross, with practically no water except occasional salt lakes, huge gravel slopes and sand hills, littered with sun-bleached animal skeletons. They passed the old landmark of the Solitary or Dry Tree, believed to have marked the final battle between Darius of Persia and Alexander the Great.

The Polos at Hormuz on the Persian Gulf. The ships they were offered were already overloaded with an elephant, horse and a camel, and very unseaworthy.
Bibliotheque Nationale Paris

Assassin Country

The Polos then passed into the territory Marco calls Mulehet, the land of the Assassins. A powerful, sinister man called Sheikh Alaodin, known as the Old Man of the Mountain, had reigned amid splendor in a fortified castle at Alamut south of the Caspian Sea. (1.22) Although the sect had been destroyed by Hulagu Khan's army 16 years before Marco travelled through the region, the threat of violence was still very real. Sheikh Alaodin had headed a heretical Ismaili Moslem sect, founded originally at the end of the 11th century. He ruled through convincing the simple mountain people that he was a prophet, the Vice-regent of God. He gathered around him fearless, audacious boys aged between twelve and twenty and gave them hashish, and while they were in a drugged sleep, took them into a secret garden, full of all kinds of earthly delights, wine, music and beautiful girls. The boys woke up believing that they were in Paradise and agreed to do anything the Old Man ordered, just to be allowed to stay. He trained them in the language, rites, and rituals of the marked men, then sent them off on missions of assassination, hence the corruption of hashashin to assassins. The boys were quite willing to do the will of the Old Man, believing that whether they lived or died, they would be in Paradise. There were hundreds of calculated murders including two leading Crusader lords in the Holy Land, Conrad, King of Jerusalem and Raymond, Count of Tripoli.

The Old Man of the Mountains, in the Garden of Paradise, Assassin country, where delights were offered to young men and boys in exchange for becoming killers. From Le Livre du Graunt Caam, MS Bodley 264, fol. 226 Bodleian Library, Oxford.

The three Polos rested for a considerable period in Badakhshan while Marco recovered from a severe illness, (1.26) before heading for Bukhara and Samarkand, through the mountain ranges of the Hindu Kush and the High Pamirs. It was hard going and bitterly cold. The air was very thin and they had difficulty cooking at such a high altitude. It still required 40 days of extremely arduous travel over the desolate country of Beloro with plateaus between 13,000 and 15,000 feet, and peaks 19,000 feet above sea level. They saw the wild curly-horned mountain sheep, later named *Ovis poli* after Marco Polo. (1.29) They then chose the direct but more difficult route round the southern side of the Taklamakan Desert via Kashgar, Khotan, and Pem (1.29). Here they found jasper and jade and the local custom of a woman warmly welcoming a stranger into her home, if her husband had been away for more than twenty days.

It took the Polos five exhausting days to trek across the salt flats to the town of Lop Nor, near the edge of the Great Gobi Desert. (1.36) Silk was part of the cremation rituals there, and the houses of mourning were hung with silk and cloth of gold. The Polos needed to take food for another month for both men and beasts to cross the desert to Dunhuang. Marco writes of hallucinations, heat haze, phantom desert sounds of wailing, drum beats, spirit voices, and attacking robbers. There was also the danger of falling asleep and going round in circles. Each evening before they settled for the night, they put up a flag so they would set out in the right direction the next morning through the formless landscape. (1.36)

Finally they reached the Caves of the Thousand Buddhas at Dunhuang, which Marco described as 'abbeys and monasteries full of all kinds of idols, to which they (the inhabitants) offer great sacrifices, and pay great honour and worship.' In the 19th century, the explorer-missionaries Francesca French and Mildred Cable called it the 'art gallery of the desert'.

The Caves at Dunhuang

The Mogao Caves are near the Singing Sands, 25 kilometres southeast of Dunhuang. In 366 AD the monk Lo-tsun had a vision of rays of light, shining like a thousand Buddhas in a cloud of glory. The monk encouraged a rich and pious pilgrim to have a cave painted by a local artist, and then dedicated to the Buddha as a shrine and to his own safe return. Other travellers, exhausted and frightened by the dangers of travel across the arid deserts, sought protection by following suit. Before long there were about a thousand decorated caves, although only 469 now remain. It became a centre for worship, with temples and valuable artifacts.

Around 1000 AD some of the treasures were walled up in a secret cave, probably to save the sacred Buddhist texts from falling into the hands of the barbarians. In 1908, the explorer Marc Aurel Stein bribed the caretaker, Abbot Wang Yuan-lu, into opening the hidden cave, known as Cave Number 17. Inside was a priceless hoard of over 50,000 manuscripts, written in many different languages, including Sanskrit, Chinese, Sogdian, Tibetan and Uighur. There were exquisite embroideries and carved figures as well, all dated to between 400 and 900 AD. It was the find of the century, a treasure trove.

Abbot Wang and the Caves of the Thousand Buddhas at Magao 25kms from Dunhuang.
In 1908 Marc Aurel Stein persuaded him to open up Cave 17.

Some of the 300 Buddhist paintings were temple banners with broad floating streamers on the sides, so long they could hang from the cliff tops above the caves. Many had a single sacred figure or

Bodhisattva, Buddha himself, Lokapalas or 'Guardian of the World' depicted on them. The votive hangings were painted on incredibly fine silk gauze, silk brocade or paper, mounted on a backing of cloth or paper and carefully patched and darned. Other sacred hangings featured a group of divine figures or scenes from the Buddhist heaven. Aurel Stein had 24 cases of manuscripts and five of paintings and embroideries and similar art relics packed and sent back to the British Museum. The silk scrolls and banners, long squashed under bundles of manuscripts had become compressed, almost impossible to open. It took British Museum staff years to meticulously unfold them and reveal their secrets.

The Polos continued their journey. Marco was interested in everything he saw, including asbestos at Ghinghintalas near Kara Khoja. (1.39) It was found as a vein in the mountain, and the woolly fibres were dried, pounded, washed and finally spun and woven under the strict control of the Khan's officers. Marco was amazed that it was cleaned by just throwing it in the fire. He mentioned also the 'stones that burn like logs' although coal was known in Europe at the time. He was impressed by the first and second class Imperial Postal Service, and the facility for top priority dispatches, not seen in Europe since the fall of the Roman Empire. He approved of the number of baths taken daily and the oriental obsession with cleanliness, and observed the wide use of paper money and the concept of credit.

Several times each year the merchants arrived in the capital city with their caravans stuffed with silks and other precious commodities. (2.17) These items were examined, a value assigned to them and then exchanged for paper money which had been made out of mulberry bark in the Khan's mint. The black fibrous inner layer was removed and glue added to the pounded bark before it was rolled out into a kind of paper. It was then cut into squares and rectangles equivalent to half a Venetian silver groat. Bigger ones were worth a groat, and others equaled five and ten groats, up to one, two and ten bezants. Special officials wrote their names on the notes and authenticated them by stamping them with the Great Khan's seal sprinkled with vermilion pigment. There were severe punishments for anyone found forging the paper money. Marco thought this was how the Khan had become so unimaginably rich, he could just make money. He was not aware that the treasury had to be backed up by real silver and gold.

A sketch of Kublai Khan as reprinted in Henry Yule's 1874 edition of The Book of Ser Marco Polo.

Kublai Khan and his Household

After crossing the deserts the Polos finally arrived in May 1275 to a warm welcome and the comforts of the Khan's great summer hunting palace at Shang-tu, immortalized by Samuel Taylor Coleridge as Xanadu. Marco was impressed by this temporary palace, cleverly made with spliced cane struts, silken guy-ropes, weatherproofed felt and lined with furs and costly silks. (1.57) It was a palace inside the royal estate, and included 16 miles of enclosed parkland, stocked with deer, gerfalcons and other game, even a tame cheetah. Everything was luxurious, exceeding anything they had seen in the West. The walls of his main palace at Khanbalik were also covered with gold and silver, decorated with pictures of dragons, birds and horsemen. There were exquisite textiles and beautiful silk carpets of many colours (2.26), and the main hall was so vast 6,000 men could dine there together.

Marco became completely overwhelmed by the numbers. The Khan had an enormous entourage of over 10,000 people to be accommodated. He had four Empresses, each with their own courts of 300 ladies in waiting, and 22 sons by these wives. (2.4) As well, there were his carefully chosen concubines, giving him another 25 sons, also groomed for government. (2.5) There were pages, servants, eunuchs, actors, musicians, court officials and physicians, along with 200 or more new concubines added every other year from the Province of Ungut. (2.4) In addition, there were 25,000 prostitutes to service the visiting ambassadors, and all had to be appropriately clothed. (2.7) This required unlimited amounts of silk and other beautiful fabrics, and in the court workshops, the tailors and seamstresses were kept extremely busy.

In addition, there was the Khan's private guard of 12,000 Barons (2.9) who needed embroidered gowns, one for each of the 13 solemn feast days of the lunar year, a total of 156,000 garments, replaced every ten years. The Great Khan's 13 special Lunar Festival outfits were made of even richer material and emblazoned with even finer jewels. For the New Year celebrations in February everyone wore white, considered a lucky colour. People brought the Khan costly gifts of gold, silver, precious jewels, pearls, white horses and lengths of white silk. Even his 5,000 elephants, walking in procession, had tented housings on their backs covered with birds and beasts embroidered in silk. (2.12) The Khan was born on the 28th September 1214 and for his birthday celebrations each year he wore his best robe of silk cloth of gold with a priceless gold belt. (2.11) The 1,200 members of his council wore similar garments of gold-coloured silk with fine leather boots and a girdle of chamois leather, all embroidered with gold and silver thread. Some garments were worth up to 1000 bezants each. (2.11)

The city of Khanbalik was one of the greatest mercantile cities in the eastern world. At least 1000 cartloads of raw silk, gold tissue and silks of various kinds were sent there every day, and traders came to buy and sell. (2.17) The rich were dressed in sumptuous, valuable clothes of silk and gold with precious furs of ermine, sable, squirrel and fox. (1.48) The poor did not wear silk, but were tithed one tenth of their income or worked one day a week to process silk, wool or hemp. This woven cloth was stored or distributed as gifts to envoys or dependants or sent to clothe the troops. (2.24)

The Khan noted Marco's intelligence, discretion and ability with languages, and sent him to most parts of the Mongol Empire, including many of the thriving centres of sericulture and the silk trade. Marco came back with a full account of the business, and lots of interesting stories and anecdotes which delighted the Khan. Marco learnt to speak Mongol, Turkish and Persian and had a smattering of Chinese but could not read it.

Marco's first mission for the Khan took over four months. First he went to Gouza where gold tissue was manufactured, (2.28) and then on to Cho-chau which produced cloths of silk and gold and a thin rich silk called sendal. Ten days ride from Cho-chau, he visited the Kingdom of Tái-Yuan-Fu and noted the many mulberry trees and the vast amount of silk produced there. (2.28) A further seven days journey west took him to the city of Píng-yang-fu, which was crowded with merchants. There the people lived by trading the silk they produced. (2.30) There was also a thriving silk industry and commerce in silk around Cuncun, where the ginger and silk products were ferried down the Kara-moran or Yellow River.(2.32) Two days further to Ka-chan-fu (Cachanfu), (2.33) there was another silk manufacturing centre with many artisans' shops and factories producing silken cloth and gold tissue of every kind. Within three days journeying, there were many more cities and towns including Ken-zan-fu, (2.34) all engaged in the silk industry.

At Vochan (2.41) Marco noted the customs of tattooing the body, gold fillings in the teeth and the father taking his new-born baby to bed for forty days, because the mother had already cared for it for the last nine months, a practice known as couvade. All the business and trade were done by the women; the men were the hunters. He found that silver was worth five times more than gold, and the merchants used a tally stick with notches on both sides, similar to tally sticks used in England at the time. The tally stick was split down the middle and each party kept half, as record and proof. There were some omissions from Marco's account as there was no mention of women's bound feet, cormorant fishing or tea drinking although he visited tea growing areas. Perhaps he had grown accustomed to these things, and just took them for granted.

Marco became the eyes and ears of the Khan, visiting the cities of Chin-ti-gui (2.49) and Chang-li (2.51), where manufactured silk was exported and sent down the river. Pazan-fu had abundant silk, (2.49) including woven tissues of gold and very fine scarves. (2.49) After six days of travelling, he arrived at Tudin-fu, which had been a major centre for the collection and trade of large quantities of beautiful silks before the city was subjugated by the Khan. (2.52) Marco then went to the province of Shantung, which he called Manji. (2.57). In the town of Pau-ghin there was a great deal of silk and woven gold tissue, as there was in Nan-ghin and (2.59) Sa-yan-fu. He said Chan-ghian-fu (2.65) produced the finest quality raw silk mixed with gold. (2.62) Four days later he arrived at Tin-gui-gui, a city famous for its raw silk. (2.66) He was impressed by the many rich merchants who lived in the magnificent city of Sin-gui (2.67) and the enormous quantities of silk manufactured there, not only for domestic consumption but also for other markets. He went on to Kue-lin-fu (2.74), where the beautiful women wore luxurious silk garments made in the district. The city of Unguen (2.75) exported much of the silk produced in this rich silk growing region. Finally he went to Pagan, before returning to Khanbalik by a roundabout route.

Marco went on many trips for the Khan. He obviously loved the fabulous city of Kinsai, now Hangchow (2.68), the intellectual centre of old China in the Sung period. It was the repository of literature, poetry, essays and printed books, two hundred years before

Princess Kokachin, a Persian miniature of what it was thought she would look like, reproduced in Henry Yule's 1874 edition of The Book of Ser Marco Polo.

Europe discovered movable type. Marco noticed everything, including the luxurious silk clothes produced there and worn by the inhabitants. Even the carriages and barges on the river were lined with silk. He noted the funeral custom of throwing silk wrought with gold onto the burning pyre. He went south to Kara-jang in Yunnan province near Burma, which he called 'Tibet,' where elephants were used in battle. He then goes on to describe the camel hair, silk and gold woven in Tibet, and the trade in sendal and other silks and cloth of gold at Ho-Kien-Fu.

After 17 years in China, the Polo brothers longed to see Venice again but doubted if the Khan, now in his 70s, would ever let them go home. They had been very privileged, but could not be sure of their continued protection under a new ruler. In 1290, when Marco returned from India, the Polos saw their chance to leave by offering to escort Princess Kokachin, a daughter of the royal household and the new bride for Arghun, the Ilkan of Persia. The Khan let them go reluctantly but with good grace. He fitted out their party lavishly, gave them letters and gifts for the Pope and passports stamped with gold.

In 1292 Marco was still only 38 years old, but by now Niccolo and Matteo were old men. The three Polos and the wedding party, including three envoys and a large suite of attendants, set off from the busy port of Zaiton in 14 great Chinese junks, five of which were large enough to require crews of 260 men. It took them 21 months to sail to the Persian Gulf, only to find that Arghun Khan had died and his brother Kaihatu had usurped the throne. The Polos had grown very fond of the Princess and were concerned about her safety and happiness, so after discussion with her she was given in marriage to Arghun's son, Prince Ghazan. He was at the time patrolling the marshes, near the region of the Solitary or Dry Tree in the province of Timochain. Ghazan seems to have been short and stocky and a fierce warrior, but very kind, and he loved Kokachin dearly. The Polos stayed a further nine months and it was during this time in 1294 that they received the sad news that Kublai Khan had died, at the advanced age of 80 years. Things turned out well for Ghazan, with a happy marriage and eventually, rightful accession to the throne.

The Khan gives the Polos a golden tablet before they accompany the Princess Kockachin and return to Venice.
Bodleian Library

Marco Polo dictating his story to Rusticello of Pisa, as reprinted in Henry Yule's 1874 edition of The Book of Ser Marco Polo.

Return to Venice

Rather than heading for the Mediterranean, the Polos travelled north to the port of Trebizond on the Black Sea and took a ship, arriving in Venice in 1295. After 23 years, they were not recognized and were turned away as tramps, so they decided to give a great banquet and invite all their family and old friends. At each course they put on another layer of their Tartar finery, ending with the rough travelling clothes. Finally, with a flourish, they ripped them open at the seams and out tumbled the gorgeous gems, hidden within the lining.

The story does not end there, for in 1298, Marco was made a 'gentleman commander' on a galley involved in yet another skirmish between Genoa and Venice. He was captured and put in jail where he shared a cell with a scribe. Rusticello of Pisa was so enthralled by his adventures that Marco sent to Venice for his notes and diaries and Rusticello wrote the stories down as Marco related them. Marco was released after a treaty was signed in May 1299; and *The Travels of Marco Polo* appeared not long after and were a resounding success. Marco married Donata and had three daughters, Fantina, Bellela and Moreta. After the deaths of his father and uncle, he continued to trade on his own account and his name appeared in various court records. In 1305 he was mentioned as 'Nobilis Marcus Polo Milioni' standing surety for a wine smuggler. In 1311 he sued a dishonest agent who owed him money on a sale of musk, and in 1323 he was in dispute over a party wall. While he led an interesting life after his return to Venice, judging by his nick-name, il Milioni, which he acquired from his constant retelling of his fantastic tales, it would seem that his life was now but a pale shadow of his years at the court of the Great Kublai Khan. He died in 1324 aged 70 years and left his fortune to his daughters. On his deathbed Marco maintained that he had told not one half of what he had really seen. He did in fact include many tall stories, but much is surprisingly accurate, and later travellers like Marc Aurel Stein and Sven Hedin have discovered places that accurately match Marco's description.

The Various Versions of Marco's Travels

There are 85 manuscript copies of the *Travels of Marco Polo*, written in Latin, Italian and French and 75 editions in 12 languages; all vary. None of Rusticello's original manuscripts still exists and none of the extant versions is complete. Rusticello wrote in French, though Ramusio, one of the translators, says he wrote in Latin. Rumusio's Italian edition (R) contains the fullest account. A Paris manuscript (F) is considered to be nearest the original, (L) is a Latin compendium and (V) is a corrupt version in the Venetian dialect. Ronald Latham's *The Travels of Marco Polo* was based on Professor Benedetto's Latin edition (Z). An Italian edition by Daniele Ponchireli with a preface by Sergio Solmi (Torino 1954) is based on a Paris manuscript. There are many other variations, versions, translations and editions. Sir Henry Yule's translation and revision of 1871 has been used extensively by other scholars and is valuable for its notes.

The edition used here is the Everyman's edition, Dent London 1975 and the numbers in brackets refer to the three Books and the various chapters.

Camels at dawn, waiting near the Singing Sands at Magao, 25 kms from Dunhuang.

Doubting Thomas, one of the scenes from the Syon cope.
The air of pathos, large expressive black rimmed eyes, stripy hair and great attention to muscular construction
render these embroideries truly acupictura, *like painting with a needle.*
With permission of the V&A Museum, London.

Chapter 4
Opus Anglicanum,
Medieval Silk Embroideries

The Golden Age of English Embroidery: what a magic picture that paints of medieval women sitting at their embroidery making the most exquisite items for themselves and the church. Silk was always expensive, so embroidery was a way to enhance plain silk fabric and add even more value. The spread of Christianity to Britain from the fourth century and improved communications with Rome, where supplies of silk were available, had heightened the desire to import silk to embellish the Church and court. The possession of these beautiful items was seen as an outward and visible sign of wealth, distinction and power.

Silk was always imported into England, because sericulture was never successfully established there. Silk arrived as small bolts or lengths of woven fabric to sew or embroider, or as raw silk to be spun into thread for embroidery, braid weaving or net making. The Middle Ages was an intensely Christian era and so a pictorial style of embroidery developed, based on the Holy Family and the lives of the saints, birds, flowers and animals, designs similar to those depicted in illuminated manuscripts and stained glass windows. The

A woman of around 1280, depicted as Eve spinning. She wears a linen hat with a wimple under the chin, pinned up on top of her head and covered with a net. Her kirtle was loose fitting, with added braid at the hem.
from Add. 38116 ff 8b 13.

fine split stitches were minute and the use of subtly dyed silk floss enabled the embroideries to exhibit great sensitivity and tenderness. Fine stitches, underside couching, brick and satin stitch often completely covered the ground of the fabric, and designs could be enhanced with additional goldwork and gems. This time-consuming embroidery using the finest silk and mostly in the service of the Church came to be known as English Work, Opus Anglicanum.

Silk was a luxury item and because of its cost and scarcity was the preserve of wealthy, leisured noble women. Spinning silk and doing embroidery were womanly accomplishments, symbolic of their status, an added refinement; not to earn their living but to enhance their reputation as the elegant lady of the manor or as a desirable marriage prospect. It was usual for noble parents to place their daughters in the household of their feudal lord or sovereign to be educated and trained in the feminine arts necessary for their status in life. Walter de Biblesworth, writing in 1300, tells how the little heiress Diane de Montchesney was tidied and coiffed after supper and taught to embroider with silk, under the direction of her tutoress.

Owning and being able to embroider silk had great prestige, as valuable as owning land. Bede describes how the first Abbot of Wearmouth made his fifth trip to Rome in 685 AD and brought back with him two large exotic silk scarves or palls. The sale of these exquisite items must have realised a vast sum because it was sufficient to enable him to purchase the land of three families at the mouth of the River Wear, for the site of his new monastic community. An Anglo-Saxon sheriff of Buckingham was prepared to grant a woman called Alwid two hides of land, provided she taught his daughter to embroider. The ability to do refined embroidery was a necessary skill if your daughter was to marry well and you and your family were to go up in the world. Denbart, when he was the Bishop of Durham, granted for life the income of a farm of 200 hundred acres to an embroideress called Eanswitha, in exchange for repairing and maintaining the clergy's vestments. The 1086 Doomsday survey of land holdings has references to skilled embroideresses, including Aelfgyd and Leofgyd. Leofgyd was a *servientes regis,* a lowly English widow, yet she had stature and some importance because she held three and a half hides of land at Knook and did gold embroidery for the King and Queen.

Silk and embroidery are sometimes mentioned in early records although very few actual examples remain. One of the earliest finds, dated during the Roman occupation of Britain around 250 AD, is a fragment of silk twill from a child's grave at Holeborough in Kent, while another came from a fourth century grave at Colchester. This was a dull, rough piece of woven 'grege' silk with the gum still in it, probably originally from China. A seventh century child's relic box at Updown cemetery also contained silk threads. There is something gentle, protective and cherishing about silk, so when a child died, tucking a tiny precious fragment into the little coffin was one of the last loving things a grieving parent could do.

Embroidering silk was considered an honourable task for pious noble women. St Etheldreda, who died in 679, made an exquisite stole and maniple, embroidered with gold and precious stones, while she was Abbess of Ely, which she offered to St Cuthbert (c 635-87). They might be similar to another set which Queen Aelfflaed, wife of King Edward the Elder, commissioned between 909 and 916 for the use of Bishop Frithstan of Winchester. This set was also gifted to St Cuthbert's tomb and parts are still extant and preserved at Durham Cathedral. These treasured items are worked in gold and coloured silk floss on silk fabric and feature prophets, clergy and saints including St John the Baptist and Peter the Deacon, with birds, lions and acanthus sprays. Another Queen, Aelgifu, the second wife of Canute, designed and embroidered ecclesiastical vestments and church furnishings which Canute later presented to the Abbeys of Croyland and Romsey. Queen Edgitha (Edith), wife of Edward the Confessor (1042-66) is said to have been a dutiful wife and embroidered the rich robes that he wore at major festivals. She was skilled in '*d'or et argent brudure,*' and her skill at doing this exquisite gold and silver embroidery led William of Malmesbury to describe her as the 'perfect mistress of her needle'.

The hagiographers who wrote the lives of saints and other important people delighted in reporting a noble lady's dedication and skill. It reinforced their belief in appropriate behaviour for a royal lady, offering the work of her hands to the glory of God and the Church. One writer waxed lyrical in describing how Queen Margaret of Scotland (1045-99) had '..a chamber that was like the workshop of a heavenly artist, copes for singers, chasubles, stoles,

Nuns wore an enveloping tunic over an underdress, with no decorations, their hair and neck completely covered by a veil and wimple.

altar cloths, and other priestly vestments. Church ornaments were always to be seen, some in the course of preparation, others worthy of admiration, already completed'.

Monasticism and embroidery

The years between 1000 and 1200 were known as the high period of monasticism, when many profoundly spiritual men and women were attracted to a life of prayer and devotion within the confines of a nunnery or monastery. Thomas of Ely records that Queen Aelgiva's daughter, the Lady Aethelswitha, refused marriage and chose to enter a nunnery near Coveney. There she devoted herself to gold embroidery, which she later presented to Ely Cathedral. Thomas says she worked the silk 'with her own hands,' which suggests that she actively sewed the fabric and not just directed her maids. There is no suggestion that a noble woman had to give up her maids when she espoused a life of poverty, chastity and humility. The priority was to be free of earthly demands to give oneself fully to God and prayer.

Beautiful textiles were highly valued and gratefully received, and were an opportunity for enclosed and pious nuns like Aethelswitha and Christina of Markyate (c1123) to dedicate the work of their hands to God. Christina was a fine needlewoman and while Prioress, embroidered many beautiful things, including three mitres and a pair of 'sandals', which were probably soft indoor shoes. Abbot Robert de Goreham (1151-66) offered them to Pope Adrian IV (1154-9), and they were so beautiful that the Pope accepted them.

The cloister was one of the few options available to an aristocratic woman who did not wish to or could not marry. It required a more modest dowry than marriage, so the nunneries accepted not only daughters who desperately desired to live a life devoted to God, but also unwanted daughters, illicit daughters of priests and plain, afflicted or handicapped well-born girls. The nunneries also took in children to be educated, widows who refused to marry again and troublesome eminent women prisoners who had been told by the court to 'get thee to a nunnery'. Many women saw life in a convent as a pleasant and safe place to live, away from a demanding or violent husband and endless pregnancies. Some widowed queens chose to endow a convent, while other distinguished women seized the opportunity to realize their own ambitions and become powerful leaders of communities and controllers of their time and wealth.

Life in a convent could be very demanding if it was an enclosed order, strictly supervised and devoted to prayer and good works. For some women in less strict convents, it could be exceedingly pleasant, with little jaunts on pilgrimages or visits to their family, gossip and chatter over a glass or more of wine in the evening. There were various amusements: minstrels, dancing, embroidering costumes and preparing for the Passion Plays, mumming and enthusiastic feasting on holy days. Some women kept pets, a cow, monkeys, squirrels, rabbits, larks, and at Nevers, there was a parrot called Vert-Vert. Lady Audley, a widow who boarded at the convent of Langley, had to be chastised and stopped from taking all twelve of her little dogs into chapel, because they made such a noise and a fuss that no-one could concentrate on the psalms.

By the late 14th century, conditions in some small nunneries had become very lax. The bishops saw supervising these nunneries as a real bother. Bishop Alnwick dutifully made the rounds of the nunneries in his diocese and took each member aside to ask them searching questions about the running of the establishment. Out it all poured – the late nights, the men who visited, the wandering off, the children born to the nuns, the misuse of funds and the time spent on embroidery.

The bishops were constantly irritated by the way the women, especially the widows, paraded in their beautiful silk gowns, open at the sides and trimmed with fur. These women flaunted their silk and gold girdles and trailed their long silk veils, worn in defiance of the Rule under which they were supposed to live in a state of modesty and humility. But it had become the custom to give the nuns a dress allowance rather than provide them with clothes in common, and so they took advantage of the lenient conditions. Who could blame them for wanting to wear the fashionable and delightful clothes sent to them, or their desire to embroider something precious to give to a friend or relation. Some fashionable women in the community even shaved the hair on their temples and tucked the rest under an exotic embroidered headdress that exposed their high foreheads. It just would not do, and the bishops fumed and ranted, but to no avail. The women always managed to find ways to sweeten a life of restriction and ennui. Time was of no moment, days flowed

There were many pious noble women who chose to live within a nunnery, giving their lives to God and devoting many hours to prayer. c.1310

into months. Their families could afford to send them lengths of silk and bundles of brightly coloured silk floss and they could embroider.

Even the question of what they should embroider caused a problem, because some bishops viewed silk work with suspicion and were critical of the time spent on the fine work. They felt it all took up far too much time that should be devoted to prayer and good works, reading or singing hymns. They maintained that the women should be mending the clothes of the poor, not sewing blood-bands and little caps and bags for friends. Embroidery could only be accepted in the nunneries if it did not interfere with or distract the women from following the Rule. Some Abbesses thought the women should be doing embroidery, because idleness left an opportunity for the devil to come and make mischief.

Clare Chasuble, 1272-94. The silver-gilt threads are worked on the dark blue silk twill ground, with the central panel containing scenes of the Crucifixion, Virgin and Child, Peter and Paul and the Stoning of Stephen.
With permission of the V&A Museum, London

Although many of the women in the convents had sufficient skills and certainly did embroidery, it is unlikely that all but the largest nunneries under the patronage of the wealthiest families could afford to accept large commissions. Most nunneries were small and often poverty-stricken, especially in the later Middle Ages. The exquisite vestments and church furnishings would have required a heavy financial outlay in silk, gold and gems, as well as secure storage. Many nunneries did have extensive collections of beautiful embroideries, probably made by the enclosed women. The 1485 Records of the Benedictine monastery of Langley mentions a whole sacristy full of embroideries, including altar frontals and suits of vestments. One was black damask, embroidered with roses and stars, and another was white, embroidered with 'rede trewlyps'. They were actually 'true lover's knots', not Turkish tulips which were still unknown in England at the time.

But there was another problem. The women's embroidery was so exquisite that it became a very desirable gift for a bishop to give, perhaps even to the Pope, so time spent on embroidery was tolerated. It is not really possible to tell if the Clare chasuble, made of dark blue silk twill (1272-1294) and probably commissioned by Margaret de Clare, sometime wife of Edmund Plantagenet, nephew of King Henry III, was the work of a nunnery or of professional embroiderers. The copes given by Lanfranc, Archbishop of Canterbury (1070-89), heavy with gold thread and embroidered with dragons and strange birds, were probably made by male embroiderers within Christ Church or by secular male professionals. It was usually men's names that were registered as designers, agents, patrons or embroiderers; women's work was almost always unrecorded. The Victorian and Albert Museum has the only known piece of Opus Anglicanum, apparently done by a woman in a nunnery. It is an altar frontal, dated 1290-1340, with the words DOMNA IOHANNA BEVERLAI MONACA ME FECIT embroidered on the back. The words embroidered in black silk have now mostly decayed, the black dye having rotted the silk.

The Church seemed to have no objection to the use of non-religious symbols or the conversion of secular garments. In 1491 Sir Gervase Clifton instructed that 'all the altar cloths of silk, a bed of gold Bawdkyne and another bed of russet satin which belonged to… (Archbishop Boothe of York) to be delivered to make vestments' for use in various chantries in Southwell Minster. In her will written in 1083, the year she died, Matilda, Queen of William the Conqueror, wrote:

> 'I give to the Abbey of the Holy Trinity (at Caen, which
> she had founded) my tunic worked at Winchester by
> Aeldret's wife and the mantle embroidered with gold,
> which is in my chamber, to make a cope. Of my two
> golden girdles, I give that which is ornamented with
> emblems for the purpose of suspending the lamp
> before the great altar.'

The 1295 inventory of St Paul's included two copes embroidered with the startling depiction of knights fighting. The 1368 Norfolk inventory notes vestments embroidered with castles, gold crowns, silver and gold stars, flowers, mythical birds and beasts, along with the donor's monogram or coat of arms.

The value of fine English embroidery depended on the complexity of the design, finesse of its execution and quality of the metal thread, gems and silk. Handspinning gold thread and wrapping it around a core of yellow silk was a skilled occupation requiring a seven-year apprenticeship. Poor quality gold tarnished and so its quality was highly regulated by the Guilds. Top quality

Figure of Peter the Deacon, part of the set of stole and maniple given at the instigation of Queen Aelfflaed to St Cuthbert's shrine. Worked in Winchester on a silk ground in surface couching using pure gold wrapped around a silk core, split and stem stitches. (909-918)
By permission of the Dean and Chapter Durham Cathedral.

Cyprus gold thread was used in the tenth century stole and maniple from St Cuthbert's tomb. The main embroidery stitch was underside couching, which attached the gold thread to the surface, forming a little hinge on the wrong side. In later years a less effective but faster method of surface couching was used. Much of the gold thread was actually silver-gilt and was combined with pearls and other gems, making the embroidered item immensely valuable and often very heavy too. Master silk embroiderers or 'garnishers' of cloth with jewels, carried high status. They were specialised craftsmen and better paid than most embroiderers. Thomasina Parker was a 'garnisshster' and was left a gift in the draper John Parker's will.

The design and embroidery on some of the best vestments and church furnishings was so fine it was like painting with a needle and was described as *acupictura*. The saints could be identified with their attributes or symbols so the holy stories could be easily understood, even by the illiterate. The design of the figures, draperies and gestures tended to be rather stylized, with the more important people depicted larger in size. The faces had large, intense black-ringed protruding eyes, high foreheads and wavy hair worked in alternating shades of green and red or other unrealistic colours. Split stitch, tightly packed and shaded, was worked in spirals to show the contours of the face and figure. Great sensitivity was achieved in these delicate embroideries. The congregation was able to ponder on the holy mysteries as they watched the priest up at the altar, clothed in the dazzling vestments. The embroideries were designed to touch the hearts of the faithful, draw them closer to the Church and help them to identify with the life and passion of Christ and His saints.

Professional Embroiderers

The period 1250 to 1350 is known as the Golden Age of Opus Anglicanum, but it was also a period of transition. As some convents became swamped with requests and commissions, the names of professional embroiderers started to appear in the public records. Between 1239 and 1245, Mabel of Bury St Edmund's name occurs 24 times in the household accounts of Henry III (1216-72). Mabel made many items of church regalia including an offatory veil which took three years to make, chasuble, apparels, stole, farons, amice, collars and

cuffs, plus a banner for the King. He obviously trusted her judgment because he left the design of it to her. Payments were made for gold, pearls, silk and fringe and later an appraisal to establish her fee, was requested from the 'discreet men and women with a knowledge of embroidery' and 'the better workers of the City of London'. Mabel is not mentioned again until 1256 when the King visited her and commanded: 'Because Mabel of St Edmunds serves the King and Queen for a long time in the making of ecclesiastical ornaments... that the same Mabel be given six ells of cloth, appropriate to her (status), and the lining of a robe of rabbit fur'. This gift of clothes was quite usual, highly valued and most welcome.

Other master embroiderers were receiving major commissions. In 1253, Maud of Cantuaria (Canterbury) was paid for a set of embroidered apparels ordered by the King's half sister Alice de Lusignan, and Maud de Benetleye was paid £27.11s.8d for 16 broad and narrow orphreys. A little later Joan de Woburn earned 64 shillings for making two more orphreys. In 1302, Aleyse Darcy was paid 300 marks for a large cloth embroidered in gold and silk and sold to Henry de Lacy, Earl of Lincoln. Rose de Burfors, wife of a London merchant, is mentioned in the City of London records of 1317 when she was owed 100 marks by Queen Isabella for an embroidered choir cope. These are substantial contracts to named women indicating that the women were most likely professional embroiderers with apprentices and a properly set up secure workshop. They were financially able to undertake top quality work and satisfy the exacting needs of their wealthy clients.

During the thirteenth century, embroiderers and their families started to set up workshops and cluster around particular areas of the City of London. Historians Fitch, Frannson and Ekwall found family names associated with embroidery. Fitch notes textile workshops and the name Settere often occurring around the church of Mary le Bow Bred Street and All Hallows. William le Settere and John Heyroun, a 'settere', were called upon to value a silk embroidered cope. Alexander Settere in 1307 received £10 from Sir Ponces Roandi, chaplain to Master William Testa, in payment of £40 for an embroidered choir cope. Other names include 'le Seur', 'le Asseur' and 'le Setter', which Frannson suggests comes from *saietier*, the Old French word for a silk weaver, while Ekwall proposes that the word 'set' comes from Middle English '*setten*' and therefore refers to an embroiderer who sets or fixes stones or gems onto a garment. '*Seu*' is listed as the French verb to sew, working with a needle and thread, so Ralph le Seur of St Mary-at-Hill in 1288, and William le Seour of the same parish in 1291 were possibly occupational names.

With increasing requests for top quality work, agents started to look to the cities for skilled embroiderers. In the past they had seen the nunneries as a source of cheap labour, but now they realized they could control these valuable commissions themselves. In 1251 Adam de Basing was described as an embroiderer, but he was probably an agent as well as a very successful London merchant and mayor. He supplied Henry III with fabric produced by Gerard le Bas in 1250 and a coat for £14.8s, so perhaps he financed other embroiderers as well. Matthew Paris may have been obliquely referring to Adam de Basing in his *Chronica Maiorum* when he wrote in 1246:

> 'My Lord Pope (Innocent IV 1243-54) noted the embroidered gold worked orphreys of the copes of certain English priests at the Council of Lyons in 1246, and commanded that the Cistercian abbots supply him with orphreys to ornament his copes and chasubles without delay, just as if they could be got for nothing and this did not displease the London merchants who traded in these embroideries and sold them at their own price'.

Syon cope, 1300-20. When the monastery at Syon was threatened during the Dissolution, the Brigantine nuns fled to Flanders, France and finally Portugal, taking with them their precious vestments. The entire linen ground is covered with underside couching in a chevron pattern, each quartrefoil containing a saint, angel or holy scene.
With permission of the V&A Museum, London.

This sounds as if Adam de Basing, rather than the embroiderers, benefited financially from the Pope's desire for these beautiful status symbols.

The Papal Treasury and Wardrobe Accounts give valuable information about continuing acquisition, patronage and gift-giving. Pope Urban IV (1261-1264) employed an English embroiderer, Gregory of London, who was especially skilled in gold work. The 1295 Papal inventory itemizes 113 pieces of Opus Anglicanum, more than any other kind of embroidery. Edward I sent a beautiful cope to Pope Nicholas VI and around 1295 he sent another to Pope Boniface VIII, both of Opus Anglicanum, which Pope Boniface later presented to local cathedrals. Pope John XXII (1316-34) received several valuable copes as gifts from England, including one sent in 1322 by the Archbishop of Canterbury and another, richly embroidered, sent by the Bishop of Ely in 1333. Edward II and Queen Isabella sent him another one on his accession decorated with large pearls.

Setting up a large embroidery studio required access to credit, to import or purchase the silk, gold and jewels and pay the workers. The Church and State were encouraged to offer patronage to ensure that their work got priority. These workshops spawned a whole new group of businessmen, managers and financiers who were already well established as middlemen, anticipating demand, facilitating production and satisfying the greed and competition for these beautiful textiles. Security was essential as gold and jewels needed locked vaults, while special chests and caskets were required to store the bolts of silk in clean, dry conditions. Silk floss was imported in bundles and then plied and doubled by the throwsters to give a particular weight and texture to the design. The Great Wardrobe accounts of 1333 note that silk thread was very expensive at 15 shillings per pound compared with linen at only 3 shillings per pound. It was usually purchased from City mercers or Italian merchants who imported it in a wide range of colours, to match the dyed silk fabric they supplied. While the workshop probably had the embroidery frames, each worker seemed to have their own pins, needles and scissors as they are never mentioned in workshop lists.

In fourteenth century London, there were other changes in the balance of working life, with more women being employed as workers in larger workshops, rather than being independent mistresses of their craft. In 1330, three counterpanes were made

Ceremonial robe, embroidered with heraldic lions and tied with gold braid and worn over a sideless surcoat, the deep armholes and bottom edged with fur. By 1446, this surcoat was rather old fashioned, a style mostly reserved for formal court occasions.

Four small scenes of embroiderers at work, pricking and pouncing, attaching the silk to a frame, transferring the design and embroidering. Windows and a candle remind of the need for good light although the guilds tried to stop people working in the evening.

for Philippa of Hainault and Edward III for the elaborate churching ceremonials following the birth of the Black Prince. Wardrobe accounts show two artist/designers, John de Kerdyff and John de Chidelee, heading a team of 112 people. John de Kerdyff was probably in charge, as he was paid 8.1/8 pennies per day for 72 days, while John de Chidelee was only paid 6.1/4 pennies per day for the 78 days he was involved. Both men were described as a protractor, an artist or designer. The silk velvet for the counterpanes cost £72, and along with 14 pounds of gold and 16 pounds of silk thread, the total cost was £201.15s.5.3/4d, more than many medieval workers might earn in a lifetime. Of the workforce, 70 men earned 4.1/2 pennies per day, and 42 women earned 3.1/4 pennies per day, a total of £60.17s.6d per day, a vast sum of money for the time.

Some embroiderers were journeymen and women who had completed their apprenticeship but could not afford to set up on their own, while others were partly skilled. One way or another, men were paid far more than women for the same job. It was believed that a woman should earn less otherwise it would upset the balance of the partnership, where man was the leader and woman the follower. Both the Church and State promoted laws and edicts, backed by selected passages from scripture, to ensure that these views were cast in stone. The women embroiderers were as highly skilled as the men, but their pay did not reflect this. By the time they became organized into a guild, it was too late to insist on equality of wages.

A big commercial workshop required highly skilled embroiderers, and many more semi-skilled workers, tailors and seamstresses experienced in working with silk. Sometimes artists like John le

Bonde and John de Stebenhethe worked together to supervise a large group. In 1308 they were described as Brouderers, but what is less clear is whether they actually picked up a needle or just supervised their workers. Sometimes, known artists like the two expert illuminators, Dame Margot and Dame Aales, were commissioned to design embroidery, but many master embroiderers probably did the designs as well. St Dunstan (c909-88), Archbishop of Canterbury, was an expert designer and was often called upon to design special vestments, but his regular visits to a pious woman called Eadelthrym to offer guidance caused some caustic comment.

The iconography used to identify particular saints and holy stories was universal, and a good artist could take these common elements, and combine them afresh to fit the current style and requirements as requested by the patron. Pattern books were available, and were used over quite long periods by artists designing vestments and domestic furnishings. One dates from around 1280 and was still in use towards the end of the fourteenth century. Inspiration came not only from the Book of Revelation, popular saints, the Apocrypha and the Life of the Virgin Mary, but also from everyday life and current literature, scenes from medieval romances, Knights of the Round Table and hunting scenes, or a pun on the donor's name: a glove for the Glover family. Patterns included interlacing, acanthus, flowers, banderoles, inscriptions and mottoes, using both religious and secular motifs.

It was a chivalric age, a time of crusades and romantic ideals. Coats of arms and other signs and symbols of heraldry were used to give quick recognition on the battlefield or at tournaments. Sometimes symbols were used on ecclesiastical items, like the small repeating rampant lions on the Clare Chasuble (1272-94) and the John of Thanet panel (1300-20). The symbols were embroidered onto surcoats, horse trappings, banners and pennons, carried by the knights. Fashionable ladies carried tiny sheer silk banners called *orifammes,* embroidered on both sides with a picture of the Virgin Mary or a likeness of themselves, a style of embroidery known as *a deux endroit.* Late in the fourteenth century, Gile Davynell earned over £700 for embroidering a jupon or military coat for the Black Prince, along with some other items. Embroiderers who could execute superior heraldic work could name their price and gain great prestige and profit.

The Great Period of Opus Anglicanum was passing and gradually and imperceptibly from the mid-thirteen-hundreds onwards,

Lady ceremoniously offers the knight his helm before he leaves for the Crusades. Over his armour he wears a tabard with his family insignia. A wealthy family would commission embroiderers, but the need for speed meant that many designs were stenciled or painted on the fabric.
Codex Manesse, Universitsbibliothek, Heidelberg, Cod. Pal. Germ. 848, f82v c1330.

standards of craftsmanship began to deteriorate. This was due to the pressure put on the embroiderers by impatient and demanding clients, social and economic stress and the prolonged, expensive, civil and foreign wars of the later fourteenth and fifteenth centuries. Many highly skilled people died during the Black Death and those that did survive often moved away or settled in other districts, so studios broke up and skills were lost. Church embroidery became formulaic, repeating a conventional design or motif, the pineapple, angels or fleur-de-lis. Production became geared to a price, and mass production methods and shortcuts were adopted in the large workshops. Stenciling or painting on a design was much faster and cheaper to produce than fine embroidery, and so was used on wall, bed and horse covers, banners and clothes, like those depicted in the Luttrell Psalter (1335-40).

Changes in taste and a growing commercial sophistication, along with great advances in the manufacture of exquisite woven damasks, velvets, cloth of gold and other luxurious woven silks, meant that rich imported broad loom silks became very fashionable and sought after. Many semi-skilled embroiderers were now working in dire conditions, crouched over long tables in poor light and unhealthy surroundings, producing little stacks of standard designs of saints and flowers, scenes from scripture and holy stories. These embroidered slips were produced in their hundreds and available for a patron to just choose from stock. The slips were then appliquéd onto the silk damask, and a braid edging and a light dusting of fancy stitches or perhaps a family shield were added to personalize the item and tie the design together, as in the Erpingham Chasuble (early 15th c). These techniques were less durable than split stitch or couching, and never so highly esteemed, and gradually both ecclesiastical and secular embroidery grew coarser. By the end of the Middle Ages, the centre of production of the finest embroidery had passed from England to the Continent.

Boccaccio, from De claris mulieribus, shows maidens picking silk cocoons off trees and weaving.
The artist knew the story of Pamphile discovering silk on the Island of Cos, but had little idea of either
a loom or the weaving process. Royal 16GV fol. 54v.
With permission of the British Library.

Chapter 5
The Business of Silk,
the Medieval Silkwomen

The silkwomen of London were real women with personalities, achievements, anxieties and ambitions. Their actual correspondence in some cases can still be read, their signature on deeds still clear and firm. It was a smallish world. They lived in the same area, and married within their close circle of friends, neighbours and associates. They stood surety for each other, were godparents to each other's children, helped one another with large orders and joined together to protect themselves, even petitioning the King when they felt their livelihood was being threatened.

Some London women took the opportunity to get into a luxury trade, by turning their domestic skill for spinning wool into spinning silk, a high value item for the increasingly exotic needs and demands of the rising city merchants, the court and the Church. Silk was then given added value by weaving it into narrow ribbons and braids, wrapping it with gold to make thread for embroidery and making it into fashion items, hats, gloves, purses, hairnets, fringes and tassels. Some women took the imported silk fabric and embroidered it with silk floss to make bags, alms purses and gifts. Working with silk was considered highly skilled women's work, and a prestigious craft.

A successful silkwoman wearing a supertunic over her long sleeved and buttoned kirtle, a decorated girdle showing at the waist. Her hat was a goffered linen band with a wimple pinned under her chin and a net enclosing her hair, c1260.

Most craft and merchant households were based around a married couple, their children, apprentices, servants and dependants, directed by the most senior man in the family. Women raised their children, took care of the preparation of food and clothing and assisted their husbands in their trades. Families had always worked together, cooperating and supporting each other within their domestic and parish sphere. It was a flexible and traditional division of labour.

The majority of medieval silkwomen worked the silk in their own homes, supplying other silkwomen with spun or thrown silk on order. Sometimes it was an agent who supplied the raw silk, even the equipment, spindle or spinning wheel. These silkwomen were in effect outworkers, offering their work in exchange for a small wage to supplement their family's income. They taught their daughters who also contributed to the welfare of the family as unpaid labour until they married. For the more accomplished silkwoman, it was not merely a sideline to her domestic duties; she was mistress of her craft. These silkwomen were recognised as being highly skilled craftswomen and some became very successful businesswomen, traders, importing silk, organising other workers and arranging lucrative contracts.

Successful silkwomen had real standing in the city and being apprenticed to a silk mistress improved a girl's chance to marry well. Quite a lot is known about Alice Claver. After she had completed her apprenticeship to a London silkwoman, to learn the 'misteries of sylkework', she married well, becoming the second wife of a successful mercer and guildsman, Richard Claver. Another woman described herself in the records as a throwster, experienced at twisting and plying the silk threads. Both of her husbands were wealthy goldsmiths, the later one becoming an alderman.

Business success often came from the combination of the husband's commercial ability and position in his guild and his wife's expertise and success as a silkwoman. As a member of one of the major textile craft guilds — the mercers, drapers, haberdashers, broiderers, or the prestigious goldsmiths or Merchant Adventurers — he could supply his wife with all the silk she needed, deal with the contracts, imports and exports and raise the finance. His knowledge of the City and contacts with the Italian merchants who imported the various grades of silk, meant a husband and wife could become economically powerful. Other craftspeople came to depend on them

In the 1260s a craftsman wore an overtunic, split at the sides and neck and soft leather shoes with seamed hose. On his head he wore a linen coif, tied under the chin. It was originally worn under a helmet but soon became essential headgear for all working men.

to provide them with the raw silk, and often to employ them too. John Stokton would have found it harder to rise to the highest position in the city, that of Lord Mayor of London, without his wife Elizabeth's financial support from her very successful silk business. It was very expensive for a man to be an office holder in the city or his guild. Although these powerful positions had great prestige and some minor advantages, they were unpaid.

The silkwomen formed a network of friends and colleagues and called on each other for help and advice. They all lived near the Guildhall around Soper Lane, Milk Street, Cheapside, St Lawrence Jewry and adjoining parishes. Alice Claver's closest friend, her 'gossep', was Alice Bothe, who lived near-by in the parish of St Mary Aldermanbury. A gossep indicated a more intimate and trusted friendship, often with godchildren in common. Their husbands were both mercers, handling a wide range of textiles and haberdashery. After Richard Claver died in 1456, Alice often called on William Pratte, Alice Bothe's husband, for help. There were still some areas, like raising larger amounts of finance, that were out of the range of women, even very successful businesswomen. Beatrice Fyler was another friend of Elizabeth and the two Alices. She lived near-by in

German woodcut of a woman caring for her child and guiding him in a baby walker. Printed by Heinrich Laufenberg, Augsburg 1491, in: Albert Schramm, Der Bilderschmuck der Fruhdrucke, Vol XXIII, Leipzig, 1943.

Milk Street in the parish of St Mary Magdalene with her husband Thomas Fyler, also a mercer, and their eight children. The women trusted each other's integrity and ability even to the extent of acting as executrix to each other's wills.

When she died, Beatrice left her business and £50 to her eldest son Edward and £30 to each of her unmarried daughters, but Edward died soon after. In his will he left bequests to a number of women, probably former apprentices or employees of Beatrice, including Catherine Sergeaunt, 20 shillings, Alice Andrew, 20 shillings, Anne Dolfynby, 10 shillings and Joan Stokes, £4. All were carefully named and the bequests noted. Beatrice's daughter Joan Marshall, also a silkwoman, probably continued to provide work for these women who had depended upon her mother.

The work

The daughter of the house helped with the household chores and was taught by her mother to spin, contributing to the families income and standard of living until she married.

Spinning and throwing were women's work and it was rare to find a male spinner or throwster turning raw silk into yarn. A spindle was used and preferred for the finest thread, even after the spinning wheel became available during the thirteenth century. The colour and quality of the silk varied, depending on the quality of the raw silk and the skill of the spinner.

The silk weavers wove narrow wares, braid, ribbons, girdles or corses, laces and ties, cauls and nets for the hair, fringes, tassels and buttons. Cauls and other woven silk fragments have been found in London excavations, including four examples of hairnets, one from the thirteenth century, and three from the fourteenth. The later ones were made of fine handknotted silk mesh, heavy enough to support jewels and other decorations. These hairnets were made using a long narrow netting needle, usually of copper alloy with an eye at each end. A bone weaving tablet, with four holes through which threads pass to build up the pattern, was found in a Fenchurch Street deposit and offered conclusive evidence that braids had been woven in Britain since the time of the Roman occupation. Braid and ribbon making was women's work. It required little space or equipment, just a set of tablets or a small box loom with rigid heddles, through which the silk warp was threaded. There were four main types of braid: tablet woven, tabby weave, finger-looped and plaited. The silk was usually plied and then doubled up to five threads for strength. It was a popular and profitable craft and vast numbers of elaborate gold and silver braids and ribbons were made by silkwomen in their own homes, or in workshops established under the patronage of the court and Church.

Occasionally silk was knitted to make ecclesiastical gloves, though silk stockings were probably not knitted in Britain until the sixteenth century. Many women made silk fashion accessories, but major items of clothing, both secular and ecclesiastical, were made by tailors. The women were prevented from making whole garments by guild regulations, which were designed to protect men's work, though the women probably made the bed linen and clothes for their family.

The traditional way to learn a trade was to be apprenticed. When Alice Bothe came to London from Derby, she lived in the house of John Abbot in Catte Street and was probably apprenticed to his wife who was a silkwoman. Abbot was a mercer and Alice met her future husband William Pratte while he was apprenticed to Abbot. It was during these years that Alice and William began a fifty-year friendship with another mercer and future printer, William Caxton.

Apprenticeships were an integral part of city life. Some girls were apprenticed to silkwomen to learn all aspects of silk work, while others were bound to women who were distinguished in a particular area, like throwing silk or weaving corses. The girls were bound by an indenture between their parents or guardians and their future mistress. A London ordinance of the early fifteenth century states that if:

> 'Those married women that are accustomed to
> practice certain crafts in the city by themselves without
> their husbands, are to take the girl as apprentice, to
> serve them and to learn their crafts, then these
> apprentices are to be bound in service by indentures
> of apprenticeship to both the husband and the wife
> in order to follow the mistery of the wife'.

The girls came to London from as far away as Warwickshire and Yorkshire, Norfolk, Bristol, Buckinghamshire, Lincolnshire and Derby. A silk apprenticeship was usually for a term of seven to ten years, depending on the age of the girl when she was indentured. The terms were strict and she had a duty to cherish the interests of her mistress, not to waste the goods or merchandise or take them without permission, to behave well and not to frequent taverns and public houses, wander off or withdraw unlawfully from service.

The mistress in turn promised to teach her and take charge and instruct her, to chastise her 'for her own good', and to give her sufficient food, clothing, footwear, a bed, and all other suitable necessities.

Deeds don't usually mention any payment, but on one occasion in the mid-sixteenth century a plea of debt was recorded by Marjery Rippyngale for £5 against a girl for board. The girl declared it was contrary to the agreement made to her mother, which arranged for the mistress to teach her 'the crafte and misterie of a Silkewoman & sewing' wherein she was 'expert and Connyng' finding the girl 'mete and drynke and all other things convenyent.' The girl's mother was to pay 20 shillings yearly to William and Marjery Rippyngale and the girl was to do service for her board. The insistence that she do service, presumably the work of a servant, as well as pay a fee to learn her trade, suggests something rather different from the usual apprenticeship.

As well as being constantly on hand to help and learn the techniques of working with silk, the girls were often entrusted with money and sent on various errands, delivering silk and making purchases. There was a celebrated case that led to recriminations and accusations that continued for twelve years. Joan Woulbarowe maintained that her mistress Katherine Dore 'immagening sotelly

Spinner standing spinning at her spindle wheel, with a man carrying a basket of buns.
From: Royal MS. 10 E IV, f.146
Reproduced by permission of the British Library Board.

to haue hold vppon her' had forced her to remain in service when her apprenticeship had finished, and then had her imprisoned until she could pay back £12.13s.4d which Katherine maintained she was owed. Of this money, £8 was the value of silk items which Joan had delivered to two women 'custumers & werkers of ye said Katherine' who were living in Soper Lane. Katherine maintained that her apprentice had unjustly taken 'thowen sylke, vncoloued and sylke dyed' amounting to £12.4s 10d, whereas Joan stated that Katherine had long since recovered her goods. In addition Katherine said that Joan still owed her £7.10s which Joan had paid to various people 'in the tyme of her Prentyshode brought silke by the Commaundement' and for the use of her mistress. The whole business had become quite unpleasant and was in dispute over two court terms, until it was finally decided in Joan's favour.

Thankfully most apprenticeships worked well and at completion, the silkwomen had their apprentices' names formally recorded by the City of London. Some girls were greatly cherished and left items in wills. In 1456, a silkwoman called Isabel Fremely left a pair of sheets and her girdle of green silk garnished with silver to her apprentice. In her will, Agnes Brundyssch, a 'citizen and silkwoman' of London, said she released Alice Seford from the rest of her term of apprenticeship and left her some household goods as well.

A woman spinning with another carding. MS 42103, f 193 from the Luttrell Psalter 1338. Reproduced by permission of the British Library Board.

Alice Claver had a series of apprentices over thirty years, though Margaret Taillour is the only woman specifically designated as her apprentice in her will and she received 20 shillings. Elizabeth Bertram was a 'cosen' of Alice's late husband Richard and she was described as her servant, though was probably an ex-apprentice and Alice generously left her a bequest of ten marks. Elizabeth Atkynson was another 'servant', again possibly an ex-apprentice, who received the lesser amount of 53s. 4d. The official records note surprisingly few apprenticeships. Of the 123 silkwomen named in the period between 1300 and 1500, only 12 apprenticeships were registered. The silkwomen did not form a guild, so probably most arrangements were informal.

Feme Couverte de Baron and Feme Sole

Once an apprenticeship was complete and the young woman had worked for a year and a day, she was free to work on her own account. She was unlikely, however, to have the business skills or capital to marry or set up her own shop. Many young silkwomen continued to work for their former mistress for wages until they married and moved to their husband's house. From there they would usually supply an agent or work their silk on a small scale. The large capital outlay required to take premises, act as an employer with apprentices and sell both wholesale and retail was beyond the possibilities of most.

Woodcut of a marriage before a priest and witnesses, by Gunther Zainer, Augsburg 1477, in: Albert Schramm, Der Biblderschmuck der Fruhdrucke, Vol II, Leipzig, 1920.

Those silkwomen who married well, and had the financial backing and support of their husbands, would probably work as a '*feme couverte de baron*', working under the 'cover' or protection of their husbands. A woman was traditionally and in law the property of her husband, and he was financially responsible for all her debts. If the husband was a guildsman or master craftsman he could be of great assistance to his young wife as he had better access to commercial contacts, imported materials and finance.

London Chancery Proceedings note that wives who traded in the city were a normal occurrence.

An energetic and skilful silkwoman, whether single or married, could own or hire a market stall or shop and trade as a '*feme couverte de baron*'. Book III of the Liber Albus states that:

> 'If a wife, as though a single woman, rents any house or shop within the said city, she shall be bound to pay the rent of the said house or shop, and shall be impleaded and sued as a single woman, by way of debt if necessary'.

Some widows and single women, even some married women, once they could afford to present themselves before the Mayor and Aldermen and prove that they were successful, of high moral standing and financially able to honour their debts and commitments, could then apply to become a '*feme sole*', a single trader. It was a very serious step to take, to move beyond the care and protection of her husband. A London Act of 1340 again in Book III of the Liber Albus states:

> 'Where a woman *couverte de baron* follows any craft within the city by herself apart, with which the husband in no way intermeddles, such a woman should be bound as a single woman as to all that concerns her said craft. And if the husband and wife are impleaded, in such case the wife shall plead as a single woman in a Court of Record, and shall have her law and other advantages by way of plea just as a single woman. And if she is condemned, she shall be committed to prison until she shall have made satisfaction; and neither the husband nor his goods shall in such a case be charged or interfered with.'

In addition to renting a shop or place of work, a sole trader could buy and sell all types of merchandise and swear oaths in the courts. She could make contracts and act independently, as if her husband had left the country permanently, entered a religious house or died, and as though she were a single woman or widow and not merely a chattel of her husband. In the eyes of the church she was still a married woman. These privileges and advantages were entirely economic, with no political rights. The custom of male guardianship survived into the late Middle Ages and women, both single and married, like children, had no civil status, with no legal and separate existence or property of their own, until they were widowed.

In the year 1457, the Guildhall Journal records only two silkwomen who came before the Mayor of London and declared that they were sole merchants, yet both women said that they had done so for a long time. Perhaps they wanted to work on a larger scale than before and raise finance or import silk from abroad. In reality, most silkwomen probably remained '*couverte de baron*', with their husband responsible for payment of their debts though it is known that Alice Claver, Beatrice Fyler and Elizabeth Stokton were all trading as *feme sole*.

Most women trading as a *feme sole* were successful, but there were cases where a merchant had sold a considerable amount of silk to a silkwoman and had been unable to recover the debt because there was no record that she had ever been formally admitted as a sole merchant. Johanne Horne, the wife of William Horne, a saddler and Alderman of London, had used her seal and affirmed to Sir John Ffynkell, a mercer, that she was a sole merchant when, in the 1490s, she purchased silk from him, worth £56.0s.6d. Ffynkell feared that if she was not registered as a *feme sole*, then his case would follow common law, and he would not be able to reclaim the debt.

Alice Claver continued to practice her craft after her marriage and probably did so initially as a *couverte de baron* with her husband Richard's consent and support. Richard was twenty years older than Alice, and when he died within five years of their marriage his will states lovingly: 'and all waye I praye yowe, tender my wyff well for she hath ben to me a full luffyng woman en my sekeness ther God reward her en hevyn for that sche hath be to me'. It is not known for sure when Alice started trading as a *feme sole*, but probably before Richard died because he fully appreciated her ability and integrity. He named her one of the executors of his will and left her the guardianship of their little son Richard and the considerable sum of £200, along with his household goods, and 'her own goodys'.

Successful businessman, c1400 wore a long houppelande with a high neck and deep bag sleeves that doubled as a useful pocket.
The more prosperous he was the better the quality of the dyed fabric.

Imports & Exports

Raw silk was imported into London, Dover, Southampton and other British ports in many forms, including loosely wrapped bundles described as 'papers of silk', or in long wrapped skeins called fardels. There was little consistency in the size of the bundles or their weight. A fardel varied in price from £30.18s.9d to £57.12s. Leonard Conterin is known to have sold silk to eight women during one year and each fardel was of a different weight and value.

This raw silk could be further processed or sold as a finished article or as sewing silk. The Italian importers and the City merchants supplied a wide range of different silk threads, often dyed to match the silk fabric they imported. Private women like the Paston women of Norfolk, sometimes bought a fine two-ply thread for eyelets, buttonholes and topstitching. Some silk was supplied on a tube, like the 'gold of Cyprus on a pipe'. It was bought by Isabel Norman 'trading for herself in the craft of silkwoman', from a Genoese merchant through David Galganete, who acted as a broker between them. Between the 18th and 22nd years of Henry VI's reign, 23 women bought silk from foreigners, mostly the Venetians.

As well as buying silk from the London merchants, some women, probably mostly widows, did travel long distances on business. They would need to have been relatively free of home responsibilities and family demands. Competing in a bigger world required special knowledge and a sharp business acumen, capital and commitment. These silkwomen mixed with people outside their known society, and this caused some anxiety. Some men feared her experiences gave her added status and authority and could be a direct challenge to their view of themselves as the leaders in the field.

Some women, like Jane Langton, figure a number of times in Chancery Proceedings and Great Wardrobe Accounts, the King's powerful household department, as trading in larger quantities of goods. After her daughter-in-law Agnes died at the Stourbridge Fair, Jane agreed to accept responsibility for payment for corses of gold, and silk goods to the substantial value of £300.15s. Despite this assurance, the agents of the two merchants of Genoa had her arrested to ensure they were paid, but she maintained she had sufficient goods and funds to cover the debt, anyway. It was usual for families to share a debt and in 1503, not long after the problems

Both men and women wore the practical and comfortable full length houppelande. A married woman modestly wore hers buttoned up to the neck, the long sleeves of her undress covering her knuckles, and her hair covered. c1400

with the Genoese merchants, Jane Langton's son John and his second wife Elizabeth were supplying quantities of silk and other goods amounting to £101.17s.5.1/4p for members of the Royal Family. Two years later in 1505, the Great Wardrobe Account notes that they paid Jane Langton for various purchases, for the use of 'the Lady Mary'.

1 oz of 'open silk' of divers colours	16d	(possibly coloured weft threads, composed of two or three strands of unthrown silk)
1 oz of 'Twyne silk' of divers colours	16d	
1 oz of Venice gold	4s	
1 'weaving stole cum sleys pro eodem'	3s	
1 oz 'webbe silk'	16d	(possibly lightly twisted tram)
'a quarter hedelyng threde pro le webbe'	5d	(loops of filament silk that hung on the loom through which the warp threads passed)
1 oz of gold 'de damask'	5s	

Piece goods are first mentioned in connection with the Act of the 19th year of Henry VII's reign which stated that no person might import into England for sale 'eny manner of Sykle, wrought by hyt selfe or wt eny other stuffe in eny place out of this Realme, in Ribandes laces gyrdylles Corses Calles (a fine hair net) Corss of tissues or poyntes,' but gave at the same time freedom to any person, 'denzien or stranger, to import al other manner of Syklkes, as well wrought as rawe, or unwrought to sell at pleasour'.

The Silkwomen's Petitions

It was just these kinds of problems that had led the silkwomen over 100 years earlier to get together to present a petition to the Lord Mayor against a Lombard who was cornering the market for all the raw and coloured silk. Although a London Silkwomen's Guild was never formalised, the silkworkers were sufficiently organized by '… Wednesday after the Feast of St Katherine' (25 November 1368) when some 'Silkwymmen' delivered to the Mayor and Aldermen a bill. It stated that 15 days earlier a pound of raw silk (*soie crude*) was worth 14 shillings, but Nicholas Sarduche, a Lombard, by his 'crafty and evil design' had seized all the silk that he could find for sale in London and refused to sell it for less than 18 shillings. Further, 'he daily spied out all the aliens bringing such merchandise to London' and there he either commandeered the market or caused them to sell it all at a higher price than they would otherwise have done, 'to the great damage of the said women and the whole realm'. Therefore 'the complainant prayed for a remedy, that they might not have cause to complain elsewhere'.

On being questioned on the 2nd December 1368, Nicholas Sarduche maintained that his master and partners had warned him by letter that 'divers bales of silk and other merchandise' had been lost and stolen on their way to Bruges, and they thought the price of silk would rise in future and that he should buy as much silk as he could. In fact, he had bought all the silk he could find, both to sell in the city at a profit and to export abroad for resale. He was not aware that he had done anything wrong in doing so and (being an opportunist) he was willing to sell the silk to anyone at all, at 16 shillings a pound.

He was then asked by the court what quantity of silk he had bought and from whom and where it was weighed. He said he had bought 59 pounds of raw silk from Paul Penyk, a Lombard, and 80 pounds of coloured silk from Dyne Sanoche, another Lombard. He admitted that all of his silk was weighed in his own house on his own balance, and not by the common balance of the city. This caused a great upset because it was against the law not to use the City's small weighing beam, and it was widely believed that Sarduche's balance was inaccurately weighted in his favour. The court did not believe his story and he was imprisoned and his goods forfeited.

Lombards and other unspecified 'aliens' were constantly being accused of destroying the livelihood of the silkwomen by importing into England 'silk thrown Rybens, and laces falsly and decyrably wrought, and corses of silke'. Between 1455 and 1504 there were five successful petitions to protect their work against foreign competition. Silkwomen like Beatrice Fyler, Joan Marshall-Fyler, and Elizabeth Stokton probably took an active part in the politics of their craft, but Alice Claver was unlikely to have been involved in the silkwomen's petition of 1455, as her husband would have been ill by that time. The petition was repeated with few changes in 1463:

> 'Silkewomen and throwesters of the craftes and occupation of silkework within London, which be and

have been craftes of women within the same cite, of tyme that noo mynde renneth unto the contrary . . . many a wurshipfull woman . . have lyved full honourably, and theirwith many good housholdes kepte, and many gentliwomen, and other in grete nombre, . . . have been drawn under theym in lernying the same craftes. . .full vertuously unto the plesaunce of God.'

The silkwomen maintained that the Lombards and other foreigners wanted to destroy these crafts, 'and all such vertueux occupations for wymmen with yis lande'. They thought the Lombards were trying to become rich and powerful by importing ready-made silk items and controlling the price of silk, thereby taking away the silkwomen's livelihood. The silkwomen complained that they could not make the products themselves because only poor quality unwrought or raw silk was being brought into England. They asked Parliament to ask the King to ban all finished silk from coming into England, and this request was granted.

Twenty years later, men are mentioned for the first time in connection with silkwork in the petition of 1482 which says there were 'menne and women of the hole craft of Silkewerk of the Cite of London and all other Citeis, Townes, Boroghes and Vilages of this Realme of Englond.' Perhaps these were men who had taken over running the silkwomen's businesses or men who assisted wives who either found it unnecessary to trade *sole* or were not permitted to do so by their husbands. If the men were guildsmen or aldermen, their knowledge of the City would have been invaluable in petitioning the King. The alien merchants were now defined as Jews and Saracens, and an embargo was set for four years and the penalty was forfeiture.

Alice Claver seems to be typical of the energetic and responsible silkwomen of her time. It was a very busy life with a network of friends and business associates, both men and women. Her strong-mindedness made her business prosper to the extent of accepting many royal commissions over a long period. She belonged to parish fraternities, contributed to charities and made substantial gifts to her workers and ex-apprentices. Katherine Champyon was probably an ex-apprentice and was both loved and valued. She was Alice's sole executrix, and inherited the silk business and the residue of the entire estate. As a mark of respect and commitment to continuing this successful business, Katherine took the name Claver, as appears when she sold ribbons and thread to the Great Wardrobe in 1483 and 1485.

For the successful silkwoman who had a network of friends, family and men of influence, the need for a formal guild structure was not apparent. Unfortunately, forces were already at work that would result in the collapse of the silkwoman's life as she knew it.

John Lambard (d 1487) and his wife Ann, (d 1488), and six of their children.
He was a Master silk merchant, and wears his fur lined Alderman's robes, a fur
edged tunic underneath, belt and gypciere or purse at the waist.
Ann wears a fashionable headdress, fitted full-skirted dress with wide fur collar, a
pomander hanging from her belt.
Brass, by kind permission of the Parochial Church Council of St Nicholas,
Hinxworth, Herts.

Chapter 6
The Guilds and the Silkwomen

In the Middle Ages the guilds were a major institution, a power base, a means of acquiring skills, wealth and prestige. All the major crafts formed themselves into guilds to establish an apprenticeship system to train young craftsmen, control their members and enforce quality standards over all the goods produced. The craftsmen got together for mutual support and fellowship and some guilds became very powerful. The London silkwomen were unique in that they continued to function as the 'Sylkewymmen and Throwsters of the Crafts and Occupation of Silkewerk', but never formalised into a guild, and by the end of the fifteenth century they had all but disappeared.

The successive visitations of the plague from 1348 left many people dead, families depleted and traumatised. Of those who did live through it, many left their homes and villages, drawn to the towns and cities, especially London, seeking a fresh start. They were looking for work and to make their fortune, free from the entrenched restrictions of village life, tied to their lord and the land. It cannot have been easy to establish oneself in this wider world and not everyone succeeded.

A Mastercraftsman or Guildsman, wears his close-fitted cote-hardi with a low decorated belt, a mantle around his shoulders, leather soles on his fitted hose, mid 14th century.

In London the new arrivals gathered together with men working in similar trades. They joined older masters and gradually earned the right to become a member of one of the craft guilds or confraternities. The guilds created statutes and regulations with an extensive symbolism of tools, patron saints and civic pageantry, and issued regulations to cover all aspects of their trade.

As well as the craft guilds, there was another group of prosperous established businessmen who formed themselves into merchant guilds. They were prepared to pay a tax or geld to the Crown to protect their monopolies and privileges. The *Gilda Mercatoria*, ie the merchant guilds, initially included craftsmen, but later became the *Gilda Mercatorum*, guild-merchants, and limited their members to established dealers and traders in their field. Some of these guilds, companies and liveries started as parish fraternities, associations of people seeking to secure mutual support and fellowship during their life, and prayers for their souls after death. They moved in more elevated circles, with an extensive network of friends and colleagues, acquiring contacts among the hierarchy of the church and court. They developed elements of secrecy and symbolism, wore distinctive dress or livery, and fought hard to have their privileges endorsed by the court. As trade intensified, the merchants gained greater prestige and became more powerful. By the early 1300s they had become exclusive trading fraternities.

The structure and scale, limitations and opportunities for the London silk market, rested with the drive and fortune of the merchants and the middle-men of the Merchant Guilds and Livery Companies. They controlled the capital, finance, importation and distribution of the raw silk from Asia, the Middle East and Europe. From the ninth century, Byzantine silk had been traded in London and York and by the fourteenth century, London had become as important an international commercial centre for the silk trade as Venice, Genoa, Marseilles, Paris and Cologne.

In Britain wool was paramount. The Spitalfields Worshipful Company of Weavers was founded in London in 1155, and was granted a Charter by Henry II (1133-89). With its strict rules on personal, civic and social behaviour and insistence on high standards of workmanship and every aspect of the craft, it became the prototype for English Medieval Guilds. The members were weavers of wool, not silk. There is no evidence that broad loom silks were woven in London, neither the fancy satins, brocades and velvets, nor the fine gauze for veils. These were all imported from the European silk manufacturing centres, especially Venice, Lucca, Genoa and Florence. There was a brief attempt, promoted by King Edward IV (1442-83), to set up silk weaving in London. An Italian weaver, Gefferay Damico who had 'konnyng and experience of wevyng clothes of damsakes, velwettys, cloth of gold, and other clothes of sylk', was offered a house in Westminster so he could weave silk and teach these skills. This seems to have aroused suspicion and opposition from the merchants and other silk importers, and Damico was hounded and later arrested on charges of debt and trespass, which brought the experiment to an end.

The men of the prestigious Mercers Guild were ever watchful of anyone other than themselves importing silk into the country, and were especially antagonistic towards the Italians and members of the Hanseatic trading league. These foreign merchants, known as 'aliens' sometimes prospered under aristocratic patronage or church support, but the local merchants were often hostile, forcing alien merchants to deal in a particular area of the town through specific channels and brokers. In 1480, William Pratte and some of the other mercers had prepared a 'book' on the offences of the Hanse to put before the King's Council. It is most likely that William Pratte and the other husbands of the silkwomen, with their expertise in drafting reports, were also involved with drawing up the various Petitions that the silkwomen presented to the King, regarding the infringements by the aliens on their silk products.

It might be supposed that the members of the Mercers' Company were the natural protectors of the silkwomen and would have been determined to block these imported goods, but in fact silk was only one part of their business. There could even have been a conflict of interest, because some of the silkwomen were themselves silk importers competing against the mercers, though the amount involved was very small compared to that handled by the guildsmen. Some men were rather antagonistic towards the businesswomen and feared that if they led successful and public commercial lives, they would gain independent status. This, they thought, could have weakened the balance between men and women's work in the household. Some feared the loss of their place at the head of the family if their wife worked on her own account with apprentices, servants or worse, handled her own money.

Guilds were not egalitarian, they were male communities where women had little or no part. They had a strict hierarchy. The Masters had the greatest prestige. They were men who had not only completed their apprenticeships, but had also become very successful. Under them were the journeymen or bachelors, of whatever age, who had completed their apprenticeship but still worked for wages. The apprentices and the Master guildsman's family were under them. Some guilds offered wives membership as 'sisters'. They usually paid lower membership fees, were able to take part in some of the religious and social events, but were barred from wearing livery or becoming involved in any serious decision making in the guild. Some guilds had women members, wives or associates, though key guilds like the scholars, lawyers, notaries, goldsmiths and portrait painters would not admit women under any circumstances.

Many of the guildsmen in the textile trades were married to silkwomen and lived in the area near the Guildhall in the parish of St Lawrence Jewry where Alice Claver spent her widowhood. Richard Claver had lived with his first wife in the parish of St Michael Bassinshaw, near St Mary Aldermanbury, the home parish of his friends and the executors of his will, John Burton and John Stokton. Sir John Stokton was also a mercer, alderman and for a time, mayor of London, and was knighted for his part in the defense of the city against the Bastard of Fauconberg. After his death in 1473, Elizabeth Stokton married Gerard Caniziani, who was a representative of the Medici family. He was also a mercer and probably one of the silkwomen's main suppliers of Italian silk. John Norlong, Ralph Kempe and William Pratte were all mercers of middling rank and as neighbours and parishioners they helped and advised each other, supported their parish charities, witnessed each other's wills, and acted as executors. Until his death in 1486, William Pratte was very involved with his two companies: the Mercers and Merchant Adventurers, serving as warden of the Mercers and as a councilman for the ward of Cripplegate.

It was a period of upward mobility. With increasing affluence and the rise of the middle classes, it was important that all should know of a man's success. The guild Masters took every opportunity to display their frequent and ever more extravagant changes of livery. They wore outer robes of purple, scarlet or green, furred with ermine, beaver and marten. They paraded resplendent in tunics of velvet and stiff, white samite silk, with silk-lined hoods trimmed with fur or gold thread embroidery. They wore brightly coloured striped silks, silken girdles and carried silk taffeta bags and purses.

Even the lesser merchants had robes of silk edged with fur, but the Lord Mayor's regalia was the most magnificent of all: shot silk, rich velvets and cloth of gold, embellished with gold braid and jewels. Women seemed to have fewer garments than their husbands. It was the men who were the peacocks.

Widowed Businesswomen in the Silk Trade

London widows had their own privileges and obligations. As the widow of a successful London mercer, Alice Claver could continue her husband's business for life, or until she remarried, and not just for forty days, as was more usual in the rest of England. Richard's death gave her back her separate legal persona, and as a widow of a Master craftsman and freeman she was entitled to be a freewoman, a *franche homme* (*feme*) of the city, provided she did not remarry. She could join in the economic and social life of the guild, although she was excluded from their political activities, and could not vote or serve as a guild officer. She could now run her late husband's business independently after paying a fee, and supervise the shop and apprentices. She could also have her name inscribed in the civic records and her will enrolled in the Court of Hustings. When trading outside the city, she would have privileges in other towns and markets. The conflict came when she had to decide whether to remain in her late husband's trade, and abandon her silk work, or to continue as a silkwoman without the support of his guild.

Sophisticated large patterned silk velvets and damasks featuring artichokes, vine leaves and pomegranates, the choice of Mayors and Aldermen to display their wealth and success.

Widows' rights were a minefield, and they could be withdrawn for lots of reasons. The main one was her remarriage to a man who was not a member of the same guild or was a Master of another craft. The guildsmen feared that there could be a conflict of interest and worse, he might gain irregular access to her late husband's guild and be party to its secrets without the years of apprenticeship and training.

Alice Claver never remarried and remained a *feme sole* and master silkwoman in her own right. She was a widow for 33 years, so perhaps being a *mulier mercatrix sola,* a single businesswoman and trader, best suited her. Her business must have been a substantial one, and living near the Guildhall, she was ideally placed for the passing trade of rich officials, lawyers, merchants and representatives of livery companies, church and court. Her involvement in the charitable fraternities of her parish meant she knew many important, wealthy and powerful people, who were well able to afford her luxury goods.

The prestige of working for the crown would certainly have increased her business, as citizens and their wives were eager to patronise those who supplied royalty. The 1480 Great Wardrobe accounts of Edward IV (1442-83) show the range of silk goods she supplied: sewing silk, silk corses, 'streyte' or narrow ribbon, single and double laces, tassels and buttons of blue silk and gold for garnishing various books, all small luxury items. Between 1483 and 1488 she supplied even larger quantities of sewing silk, ribbons and gold fringe, purple lace and gold thread from Venice. She also supplied the decorative tassels and buttons for the coronation gloves and velvet mantles for Richard III (1483-85) and Anne, his Queen. Alice was paid 60s 7d for the white silk and gold lace to tie the Queen's mantle, worn during the coronation vigil procession through the streets of London. She was paid 2 shillings for her own labour, a very small part of the whole cost. She continued to sell silk items during Henry VII's reign (1485-1509), including 36 buttons of Venice gold at 3 pence each and six ounces of red silk ribbon for Henry's coronation robe. These were completed items, not spun or thrown silk to be further worked. This suggests that she was commissioning items from other specialist silkwomen, trading and supplying as well as producing silk fashion accessories herself.

Most silkworkers in London worked on a more modest scale than Alice and would not have been admitted to the freedom of the city. There were laws that effectively disbarred women from much commercial activity and controlled the amount of credit they could

Woodcut of a woman trader, selling clothes, some possibly secondhand. She wears a couvre-chef and apron, with a purse at her belt. A substantial stand with a mirror, suggests that this is her regular trade. Woodcut, printed by Hans Hofmann, Nuremberg, 1490, in: Albert Schramm, Der Biblderschmuck der Fruhdrucke. Vol XVIII, Leipzig, 1935.

raise. Women could have problems collecting debts owed to them. In her will, Alice left her trusted servant, Thomas Porter, £6 13s. 4d on top of his wages, with the request that he collect the debts owing to her, a task which shows the need any *feme sole* had for at least one responsible male servant, if she was to run her business successfully. It was seen as inappropriate behaviour for a woman to go around and collect money owing to her. It was much better if she was represented by a man.

For most silkwomen their work was low paid. Some women did quite well when they found they could turn their domestic skill of spinning wool into the more highly skilled and lucrative art of spinning silk. Other women found work as silk throwsters. Expert sewers made purses or coifs and those with connections to the Goldsmiths guild learnt to spin the gold around the silk to make the valuable gold thread for embroidery. Nevertheless, many women were very poor and lived from hand to mouth; some did not even own their own spindles or spinning wheels. These women paid an agent for the hire of their equipment and he supplied the silk and set the wages, so they never seemed to get out of debt. With these working conditions and the insecurities of city life, they were effectively tied to a master, not free women at all.

With so many women engaged in silkwork, it is very surprising that the London silkwomen did not form a guild. They were Master craftswomen having completed an appenticeship, and called themselves the Sylkewymmen and Throwsters of the Crafts and Occupation of Silkewerk, but in contrast to the men, they had no ordinances of their own, no sustained, formal guild structure, made no consistent attempt as a body to keep standards and consequently were never very powerful.

The women did have other options to forming their own silk guild and some joined purely religious guilds and parish fraternities. Alice and her husband Richard were both members of the Penny Brethren of St Lawrence Jewry, and she was also a Sister of the fraternity of the Founders' Company and left it 40 shillings for their prayers in her will. Richard was also a member of the Mercers' and Merchant Adventurers' fraternity of St Thomas Becket. Perhaps as a widow, Alice found the Penny Brethren at her own parish more congenial. Membership of a prestigious parish fraternity had status, and could lead one into more elevated social circles, but mostly it was just a safeguard against the demands of business failure and growing old.

Perhaps their relative independence lulled the silkwomen into a false sense of security. The successful ones already had an extensive network of friends and colleagues, so probably they did not feel the need for an additional structure. As wives or widows of guildsmen they could call on help at any time, as they did when they were presenting their Petitions to the King. Most wives had limited rights and strong associations with their husbands' guilds and were perfectly satisfied with the religious or social benefits from that.

Perhaps some silkwomen were wary of being charged with witchcraft and sorcery, as silkworking had long been a 'mistery' craft which was believed to have secret rituals and power. All the other guilds, however, had their own secret signs and initiations. A rich tradition of myths and legends grew up among women as they met to spin. Stories from the Gospels of the Distaffs *(Les Evangiles des Quenouilles)*, which connected female work with love and magic were told and retold. A spinning day could be made to foretell the future or a broken thread meant a quarrel. There were old wives' tales that said that the first man to break a thread across a doorway would be your future husband, or that fairies would come and finish the spinning, or be mischievous and tangle the thread. It was even believed, somewhat disingenuously, that it was unlucky to work on Virgin Mary's Day, Saturday.

Silk Spinning in Europe

While the English silkwomen did not form a guild, Paris and some other cities, famous for their silk, certainly did. The Paris Book of Trades, *Livre des metiers,* was drawn up and edited by the royal judge, Etienne Boileau in 1270, probably on the orders of King Louis IX (1226-1270). It contains a description of the rights and duties of 100 Parisian craft guilds including the five women's guilds, all involved with silk. The tax register, the *Livres de la taille,* of 1292 records eight female silk spinners, and by the next census in 1300 this number had risen to 36 journeywomen, *ouvrieres de soie* (workers in silk), but only one female Master silk cloth producer. It identifies the women who were actually practising their craft, and notes how women dominated in the silk trades.

Young girl with a spindle, her long surcoat pinned up at the hem, the deeply cut armholes showing her kirtle underneath. Her hair is neatly tucked up into her couvre-chef. Early 14th century.

Paris had two separate silk spinning guilds. The women who were using large spindles were professionally independent, yet were managed by two male overseers who were commissioners from the town council, *prud'hommes jures*. The small spindle spinners produced the stronger thread and this guild accepted both girls and boys as apprentices for a term of seven years, though in practice it seems only girls and women were members. Despite being a guild of women, men were brought in to oversee the guild along with the senior women.

The silkspinners were not held in particularly high esteem because they were piece-workers, and like the London women were employed by a silk mistress or agent who owned the expensive raw materials and decided the wages. Worse, the agents often avoided paying the silkworkers in cash and offered a substitute or another product, an unsatisfactory arrangement known as the truck system. Spinners were the worst off of all the silkworkers and were under-financed and unprotected by powerful husbands. Sometimes the women were accused of cheating and pawning or selling off the good quality silk the agent had given them, and substituting poor quality silk, to make a little profit on the difference. It was a hard and pitiful existence, in sharp contrast to the luxury product they handled.

The silkspinners also had competition from Beguine convents and orphanages. Convents could sell the spun silk cheaply because it had been done *gratis,* to the benefit of their house and the glory of God. An orphanage near Lyons also took advantage of cheap labour by hiring a Dame Lucresse, her name suggesting that she came from the silk city of Lucca, to teach the girls to unwind the silk from the cocoons, prepare thread and wind it onto bobbins. The older girls taught the younger ones and the programme became the next best thing to an apprenticeship for impoverished girls.

Embroidery and Silkwork in Europe

In 1303 the Provost of Paris, Guillaume de Hangest, approved the earliest known regulations of any embroiderers in Europe, although the guild was not actually registered until 1471. Paris was a sophisticated royal city, geared to offering the rich all the little luxuries of life they so enjoyed. It had a well-developed silk manufacturing trade which flourished until the late fifteenth century, and was almost unique in its attitude, accepting women Mistresses of their own guilds. The silk cap and bonnet makers functioned autonomously with their own jurors, people nominated to ensure that standards and quality of work were maintained. Their apprenticeship was for seven to eight years and the statutes allowed them to take on one female apprentice as well as family members without requiring the payment of fees. Nevertheless, like the milliners, the husbands took care of the sale of the bonnets and caps, bought the materials and supplied or arranged the capital.

The purse-makers guild, the *faiseuses d'aumendieres sarrazinoises,* made small money pouches and purses for alms. They accepted only girls for an apprenticeship of ten years, which could be reduced to six by payments. In 1299, there were 124 women, yet this women's guild was supervised by male *jures,* presumably not masters of this craft, who inspected the work for quality and enforced guild ordinances. Only one of the Paris guilds, the weavers of women's headdresses, was actually managed exclusively by the women. In all the other guilds, the women shared the power or played no role at all in governing the guild. This apparent willingness to accept a subordinate role by women in their own guild is surprising, especially in the case of the silk spinners and purse-makers, both exclusively women's guilds.

There were pockets of silkworkers in many European countries like Spain and cities and districts, including Strasbourg and Florence. Sericulture had been established in the Po valley from the tenth century and around Salerno from the eleventh. In Southern Italy, most of the work was done by Jewish, Greek and Arab immigrant families. Lucca was the first centre in Italy for the actual manufacture of silk goods, and was well established by the late twelfth century. There was a guild of women silk weavers in Zurich. They worked for distributors, but on their own account as winders, tackers and warpers in crafts supporting the weaving industry. In Lyons, working silk was a family trade, with the mother and daughters unwinding the cocoons and preparing the thread on the bobbins for the father who was the weaver. Velvet and taffeta weaving was exclusively a male job. If girls had to be hired to unwind the cocoons, as Estienette Leonarde did in 1557, the girls' wages were about half to one third that of the boys and men. One young boy, an apprentice velvet maker from Avignon, earned ten livres per year, *avec bouche, couche et chasse* (with board, room and pants).

Ann Lambard wears a fashionable butterfly or kite veil supported on wires, her hair pulled back and tucked into the rich box headdress. Her chemise shows at the neck, above a fine fur collar.
Brass, by kind permission of the Parochial Church Council of St Nicholas, Hinxworth, Herts..

The Successful Silkwomen of Cologne

The Cologne silk trade was dominated by women from the elite section of society though they did not run it. It was administered by a board, the *Seideamt,* which was founded by statute in 1437. The guilds included the yarn makers - *Garnmacherinnen*, gold spinners – *Goldspinnerinnen*, and the silk makers - *Seideweberinnen*. The silk embroiderers mainly produced heraldic embroideries, liturgical garments, bishops' mitres and ladies' bonnets. Like the other guilds, the silk dyers' charter contained numerous requirements as to quality and raw materials. The silkwomen worked very closely together within the guild structure, and this was the basis of a very successful period for Cologne silk in the second half of the fifteenth century. Between 1437 and 1504, 116 silkwomen ran their own companies. Records show that in five years, between 1491 and 1495, 100,000 pounds of raw silk were bought and processed by master silk makers in Cologne.

Many silkwomen traders and merchants travelled and were active, buying and selling at the Frankfurt Trade Fair and other big fairs. They produced high quality export goods and financed and managed their own deals. Many had their own shops and apprentices, some imported the materials they needed, but most depended on merchants to distribute their silk goods outside Cologne. These were independent women, not employed by the merchants. They had control over their products, set their own prices, and their guild had high standing in the community.

There were some very astute and successful silk families headed by women in Cologne. Tryngen Louback's mother was the silkmaker Niesgin Wyerdt, and her father, Mertyn Neven, was a successful Cologne merchant, silk trader and councillor. Tryngen's husband, Conrad Louback, was also a silk importer. As well as managing her silk business, Tryngen was involved with her husband in the wine trade, and ran his business after his death. She must have been very wealthy, because she purchased about 20,000 pounds of raw silk per annum, about a fifth of the total imported into the city. Her son, Mertyns II Ume Hove, married Lysbeth Lutzenkirchen, and they carried on the business of their parents and parents-in-law into the next century.

Lysbeth's mother was Fygen Lutzenkirchen. She was a formidable businesswoman and had been a Master silkmaker since 1474, taking on twenty-five apprentices between 1474 and 1497. Fygen's husband

A trader, possibly a silkwoman, selling gloves and bags and chatting to a customer, 1475-85.
From 'The Birth of the Virgin', the Parish Church of Kirchdorf-on-the-Krems

Peter Lutzenkirchen was a major agent for several trading houses and obtained silk from Valencia, supplied gold yarn destined for Genoa and Venice, visited the Brabant Fairs at Bergen op Zoom and Antwerp, as well as the Frankfurt Fair, and was elected to the Senate several times. Both Fygen and Peter served on the guild, term and term about, for 18 years, but after his death in 1498 she stopped her own silk activities and concentrated on his business. By 1511 Fygen Lutzenhirchen was listed as one of the richest citizens of the city.

It was not easy for all women to make a good living in the textile trades. Some guilds were able to pass very restrictive laws. The town councils of both Cologne and Constance had draconian employment regulations affecting women tailors. They ratified laws in 1426 and again in 1440 with more than a hint of male protectionism. These laws limited the seamstresses to remodelling old petticoats, and prohibited them from making the beautiful and much more prestigious and lucrative silk clothes.

While France was working to produce richly embroidered clothing for the nobility, the English production was mostly for the church. The London Broiderers Guild was a male guild, established in the fourteenth century. Some of the men are known, like Robert Ascombe who represented the Brouderers with Nicholas Halley in 1370 on the common council of London, and also worked for Richard II in 1394-8. In 1431 John Mounselle was elected mayor, probably the same man who was embroiderer to Henry VI in 1441. The men fought hard to keep out inferior work, especially embroideries sold at the fairs, and in 1423 they petitioned Henry VI to have all unsatisfactory work confiscated or burnt. The embroiderers were feeling threatened and tried to tighten their control over all aspects of their craft, but fashion was changing and it was becoming an age where quicker results were required. Superb, woven brocades were arriving from Italy and Spain, and to the embroiderers' distress, Henry IV (1399-1413) commissioned vestments not from the embroiderers of London but from the weavers of Florence.

In York between 1394 and 1551 there were 18 vestment makers, but after the Reformation and the destruction of so many churches, vestments were no longer required. Most makers became Freemen Embroiderers, doing secular work. It was part of a general trend, a further change, and much of the work was now done in commercial premises out of the control of the guilds.

The Transference of Power

By the late fifteenth century the London guildsmen had become most anxious about their prospects and position, especially as there was a down turn in economic conditions. The husbands and other men who had helped promote the various Petitions to the crown to protect the silkwomen and their work, had become increasingly involved and had taken over more and more responsibility for the everyday running of the craft. For the women, it must have been easier to let the men who were experienced in the ways of business, control access to the raw materials and production, and sale of the finished goods. The businessmen took the high-profile, high status external role in the craft, as merchants, dealers and financiers, thus acquiring public acclamation and financial rewards. There were mutterings and charges of monopoly and elitism against them, but the guildsmen persisted in promoting laws that protected and favoured themselves, to the detriment of the individual silkwomen. It became more difficult for a girl to be an apprentice, for a woman to take her on, or to run her deceased husband's business as a freewoman of London. The latent misogynism, not too far below the surface, led some men to describe the women as inferior, spiritually deficient, undisciplined and disorderly. In this climate, women were seen as second class workers and their work as women's work, of little commercial value.

The silkwomen do not seem to have protested, not because they could not agitate as they proved with the Petitions, but because in an all-women sphere of work, they did not seem to believe that they had primary rights. They had no ancient customs or guild to back them, legal statutes restricted their political power or influence, they were disbarred from raising significant amounts of finance and were probably reluctant to do anything that would jeopardise the remnants of privilege and status they still had.

Clearly this reluctance to register and defend their own guild, organise their work and take on the male-dominated guild system was devastating, because it left the silkworkers vulnerable and unprotected by a formal structure. Opportunities were lost when the women were not publicly seen together as a strong, formally organised and powerful group. There were no women role models with authority and leadership and they did not march in craft parades or wear brilliant and distinctive livery. It seems the women believed that their experience of community and co-operation would be sufficient to safeguard their place at work and in society, but it was not so. By the end of the fifteenth century, the restrictions and controls the male guildsmen had imposed, suffocated the industry to the point of decay. It took the influx of the European silk weavers into England in the late sixteenth century, for the industry to revive and flourish again.

Christine de Pisan offers Isabeau of Bavaria, Queen of France a copy of her book of poems. The women in their rich gowns in the fashionable houppelande style and high horned headdresses are surrounded by sumptuous silk textiles, wall coverings and bedhangings. Late 14th century.

Chapter 7
Silk in Fashion

The story of silk in medieval fashion was, in the end, one of availability; access to the finest fabrics and access to the credit to pay for them. It was the merchants, church and the royal court who imported silks and controlled their availability. They had the money, and they set the fashion. Luxurious silken garments were a sign of refinement, prestige and power. Silk and gold captured the imagination, turned heads and incited desire and admiration.

The late Middle Ages, for the men who could afford it, was increasingly a time of flamboyance, clothes in bright colours, richly embellished with as much gold and as many jewels as the garment could stand. It was a time of male display in the court, in the church and in the guilds. Women played a subsidiary role and were often dependent on their menfolk for gifts of fine textiles. People bought at fairs and markets. Some women had their own funds and could spend lavishly on clothes, but few had more than two or three gowns, far fewer than their men, but then, they often had their jewels.

It was the Age of Chivalry and the Crusades, a time of both exquisite refinement and calculated brutality. The knights attacked and ransacked the palaces and churches of Byzantium and brought back exotic oriental silks as booty and the spoils of war. At home,

Sketch taken from John Foxton's Liber Cosmographiae, fol.35v, The Sun. The young man wears a short rich silk houppelande with bagpipe sleeves, high neck lined with fur and long fitted hose.

the fabrics were received with wonder and delight, and they set the fashion for large, complex patterns, using metallic threads and brilliant colours, red, violet, yellow, blue and green.

Our knowledge of costume comes from written descriptions, criticism of people and their behaviour, Royal Wardrobe accounts, wills, legacies and court records, manuscripts, funereal brasses, sculpture and paintings. Very few actual garments survive except as fragments. Most clothes just wore out through repeated use and limited cleaning arrangements. Many were turned inside out and re-sewn to hide the stains and wear, or re-cut to fit a child. Finally the remaining bits were used to trim other garments, or made into quilts, mattress covers, aprons and dishcloths. It was common practice when a particularly rich garment wore out, to cut off the gems and burn the item to retrieve the gold. There was also a very lively trade in second-hand clothing; absolutely nothing was wasted.

A few precious tenth and eleventh century fragments of woven silk were found in Milk Street in London, during archaeological excavations in 1976. There were silk ribbons and some fragments of shot silk, with a different colour in the warp and weft. Four of them were tabby weave, one a 2,1 twill, but none had been woven in England. Occasionally silk items have been found in towns like York and Winchester, but it is only in the tombs of the nobles and church dignitaries that gorgeous, patterned silks are found.

The use of silk for both clothes and furnishing only affected a narrow band of society because most people only had access to locally grown wool, hemp or linen. Following fashion was an aristocratic pursuit. The ideas gradually filtered down through the general population in a diluted form and influenced the clothing of ordinary people. Clothes could instantly tell others of your occupation, religious values, rank and position in the social scale. As a result of wars, pestilence and plague, society changed and became less influenced by the strong arm of the church. Women's costume in particular was controlled by church doctrine and the insistence on the sinfulness of Eve. The church fathers defined appropriate behaviour for women and what they should wear. Women were commanded to cover their hair and conceal their bodies in enveloping mantles and gowns, and were criticized for any extravagance. Some people started to move away from their traditional place in society, to become both physically and socially mobile and to climb the social ladder. It was the fear of not being able to tell who was important that led to a rash of sumptuary legislation, to control what people could or should wear, and when.

Serving woman wearing a headscarf and loose gown, with a purse attached to the belt, taken from the Luttrell Psalter, 1340.

It gives an unbalanced account of a society not to include peasants and villagers, but wearing silk was just not financially possible for them, and there were laws to ensure that people did not dress or rise above their station. Peasants' clothes hardly changed in style. They were made of handspun and woven wool, lined with animal skins for warmth. The men wore a short tunic and braies or underpants, under another tunic. The women's chemise or shift was full length and covered by a shorter kirtle and super tunic that was hitched up when she worked. They both wore a mantle or wrap when it was cold and a hood attached to a shoulder cape called a chaperon. Later in the period, some men wore a linen coif that tied under the chin, sometimes with a straw hat over it to protect themselves from the sun. As early as 686, a West Saxon churchman called Adhelm maintained that men and women wore tunics with silk trimmed sleeves, but they would not have been peasants.

By the tenth century most men wore two tunics, the fabric reflecting their social standing. The chainse, or shirt, was made of bleached linen and the bliaut, or overshirt, which came down to the knees, was made of wool or silk. Henry II, Emperor of Germany, was the first to have a very novel addition; a pocket in his white silk damask bliaut. Most people attached their possessions to their belt, but his pocket had a vertical opening just below the neckline, and was hemmed with a wide strip of violet and blue brocaded silk, with green silk piping.

The eleventh century saw few changes in fashion. Women were simply dressed in two or three layers, a long-sleeved chemise of linen or hemp, and over that a simple kirtle and calf length tunic tied with a girdle. When it was cold, she wrapped herself in a cloak or mantle. On her feet she wore sandals or soft low-heeled leather shoes. A noble woman's gown or kirtle might be silk damask or fine wool. It fitted the hips and fell in folds to the ground. Her tunic had narrow sleeves with wide drooping cuffs, edged with embroidery or braid. Maidens wore their hair unbound, while women wore theirs in long swinging plaits, sometimes two or even four, hanging down the front and back. Plaits offered a great opportunity for a little individual style, and could be extended with horsehair, ribbons or little bells that made a tinkling sound as she walked. Sometimes women covered their plaits with long silk casings, called *fouriaux*, or wore a simple jewelled hairband.

A noble woman spinning, wearing a long sleeved chemise and over it a semi-fitted gown, wide cuffs and a long belt wrapped twice around her waist and hips. c1180

Over the short under-tunic, men wore a cote (cotte or coat) which was calf or ankle length. It was cut with magyar or dolman sleeves, decorated with bands of braid around neck and hem and belted low on the hips. The cote could be worn alone, or covered by a rectangular sleeveless surcoat, known as a tabard. It had originally been worn by the Crusader knights to stop themselves scorching in their armour in the blazing sun, while on campaign. It was split up the back or front, and could be belted or worn loose.

For women, the changes in fashion in the thirteenth century were from loose, flowing garments, to a closer fit, more 'cut'. Compared to fine wool, silk was stiff and did not drape as well, but it looked and felt wonderful. Both the tunic and gown were long, the outer garment forming a small train. Her silk or leather belt had a silver buckle and a very long tongue, which swung seductively as she walked. Sometimes she wore a fitted sleeveless super-tunic with long vertical slits for the armholes, and tucked up her skirt to show her pointed shoes. A married woman wore a stylish barbette, a band of linen worn under the chin and over the top of the head, allowing the hair to show. It was held in place by a goffered or fluted linen band or a delicate metal coronet or filet, a style made fashionable by Henry II's wife Eleanor.

Imported Silks

Luxury fabrics were available, but very expensive. Striped tabby silk was popular for linings and secular clothing as well as vestments, furnishings and bed-hangings. Velvet was initially used for furnishings and was produced by running an extra warp thread over a series of rods to form a looped pile of silk above a linen tabby base. The pile could be cut, partly cut or left uncut and was known as ciselé velvet. One of the earliest references to its use in England was in 1278 when Adinettus, Edward I's, tailor purchased it in Paris to cover the head of the King's bed, at a cost of 100 shillings. Some velvets had patterns of animals and Kufic or Naskshi script and incorporated metallic thread. The script is not unexpected as many of these beautiful fabrics came from Spain, with its tradition of Arabic weavers. Some fabrics were so gorgeous that sumptuary laws were passed so only people of the highest rank could wear them.

The arrival of three envoys from the Mongol Empire to the court of Edward II in 1307 coincided with the re-opening of trade routes to and from the East. The rich silks they brought as gifts for the King inspired a passion for oriental dress. Even William Langland in *Piers Plowman* portrays Charity as preferring 'clean rich robes of cobweb lawn and cloth of Tartary'. Twenty-four years later, at a tournament held in Cheapside in 1331, Edward III and his courtiers were dressed in the style of the Tartars. *Pannus de Tars* was presumably a silk cloth from Asia and was bought on several occasions before this event for the Great Wardrobe, the King's holding and distribution centre in the East End of London. Lovely striped, mottled and checked velvets, shot through with metallic threads, are also mentioned in the accounts.

The availability of these expensive silks, plain and patterned lampas weaves, satins and velvets, enabled the nobles and wealthy citizens to rationalize their purchases by maintaining that they were buying them as gifts for the church. They might purchase a silk cloth, *pannus de sirico de auratus,* or a piece of cloth of gold fabric, a *pannus aureus.* Often wills stipulated that the fabric was to be used as a pall, laid over the coffin for all to admire during the funeral rites and procession, before being given to the church to be made up into a vestment. In 1348, a wealthy citizen of Anze, near Lyons wanted his cloth of silk and gold made into a chasuble after his burial. A will of 1310 states: "I desire that a cloth of silk should be bought and that it should be laid over me and I give and bequeath it to the church of St Rambert". These silks were not bought to be worn but were for ostentatious display and a reminder of the donor's generosity, even after death.

In the fourteenth century there are many references to both plain and patterned silks. Velvet was still very expensive. In 1329-31, red velvet was 13s 4d per ell (an ell measures about 45 inches), while striped velvet was 10 shillings an ell in 1344 and checkered velvet 8s 4d. Lucchesse silks are mentioned in the 1388 Inventory of Westminster Abbey. It lists a set made from 'multi-coloured striped cloth of gold from Lucca, inscribed with curious letters' (*panno aureo de Luca varij coloris stragulatum et diveris literis scriptis*), given to the Abbey by Simon Langham, sometime Archbishop of Canterbury who died in 1376. Satin was widely used for all manner of clothing: doublets, tunics, hanselyns and sloppes, girdles and garters. Blue and green, black, white and red were all fashionable colours in England at the

Silk and gold damasks and velvet, with large naturalist patterns featuring fruit, flowers and birds. Many valuable silk fabrics were made in Lucca, Genoa and Florence in the 14th century.

time. Furnishings included cushions and bed-hangings, embroidered in gold or silver gilt, or decorated with painted or stenciled designs that were quicker and cheaper to produce than either embroidery or woven fabric. Chaucer mentions silk and satin, as he paints a picture of luxury and ease in his *Canterbury Tales* (c1387-1400).

> I woll gyve him a fether bed
> Rayed with golde and ryght well cled
> In fyne black sattyn doutremere
> And many a pylow and every bere
> Of cloth of Raynes to slepe on softe
> Hym there not nede to turn ofte

Fourteenth Century Fashions and the Cote-hardi

Lady with plaited hair wearing a cote-hardi. It had tightly buttoned sleeves with long floating tippets attached around the upper arm. The openings called fitchets on the front of the skirt allowed her to get at her purse, attached to the belt of her underdress. 1364

Edward III had a long reign of 50 years, from 1327 to 1377. He was born in 1312 and in 1328 he married Philippa of Hainault. She brought with her, not only numerous courtiers and ladies-in-waiting but also new ideas in fashion, loving support for her husband and a good deal of common sense. It was a more fashion-conscious age and courtiers competed for the latest fashion items and accessories. Philippa was certainly extravagant and loved beautiful clothes and furnishings. She ordered her tailor, William de London, to make a 'robe' of five garments of purple velvet, for her churching ceremonies after the birth of Edward, the Black Prince in 1330. The King's armourer, John of Cologne, was responsible for the embroidery, including the golden squirrels. The whole set or suit of garments needed 162 ells of fabric, 14 pounds of gold and 16 pounds of silk thread. In addition, John needed to purchase extra hooks, cord and thread. The total weight of the garments was daunting and the cost was far more than many people would have earned in a lifetime. Philippa later donated her squirrel robe to Ely Cathedral and it was so vast that between 1321 and 1341 it was cut up and made into three copes for the use of John Crauden, the Prior of Ely.

In 1332 William of London provided Queen Philippa with 13 matching sets of garments, a total of 55 individual pieces plus extra hoods and other items, for her to wear at the great feasts, including

All Saints and St Mary Magdalene. Her total of 71 garments was less than King Edward's 60-100 new garments each year. He also required gear for jousting and other sports, heraldic flags and banners, tunics and hangings, most of which were supplied by his armourers. They were later responsible for embroidering the Black Prince's jupon, its replica still on display in Canterbury Cathedral.

The most notable fashion change during the fourteenth century was the acceptance of the smooth fitting cote-hardi. This garment, with variations, was worn by both men and women after 1330. Its figure-hugging shape extended for men to the knees and then flared out to the floor for women. It needed buttons or lacing down the narrow sleeves and centre front to ensure a good fit. The long flowing bands and streamers attached to the upper arm, known as tippets, became so long they had to be knotted at the end, to stop them from dragging on the floor. The edges were dagged or scalloped, initially a male prerogative, and cut into interesting leafy designs. The heraldic theme continued and the cote-hardi was sometimes parti-coloured, halved or quartered, diagonally striped or rayed. It was all in keeping with the long pointed shoes called poulaine or cracowe, named after the city from where they apparently originated. They enraged some members of the church and, in France, Charles V (1337-80) condemned them as a 'deformity, thought up as a mockery of God and His Holy Church'.

Wealthy women paraded in their silk damask cote-hardi. It was flared and gored and probably cut on the bias. Its smooth fit over the bust and hips leant itself to the swaying walk that was universally admired. Sometimes it had little slits in the front, called fitchets, so the lady could get at her embroidered silk alms purse hanging on the belt around the waist of her undergown, where it was protected from 'cut-purses' and other vagabonds who might steal it. The super-tunic of the 1350s had deep curved armholes, edged with fur. This graceful style allowed the kirtle or cote-hardi to be seen underneath, and the lovely silk girdle worn on the hips. An especially rich and beautiful girdle might be a gift from a husband or lover. One writer advised that the fur trim should be removed in the summer months, because it attracted fleas. In fact a little flea band was sometimes worn on the wrist for just that purpose.

Necklines got lower and wider, exposing bare shoulders. Older women wore a fine linen wimple, draped under the chin, covering the neck and tucked into the scooped neckline, and topped by a shoulder-length veil, fluted at the edge. Plaited hair was now looped

Prosperous craftsman wearing a smoothly fitted, buttoned cote-hardi and shoulder cape with attached hood and a long liripipe called a chaperon. With his fitted hose he wears soft flat slightly pointed shoes, c1360.

up at sides of the face in front of the ears, and covered with a net or crespine. Chaperons continued to be worn outdoors by both men and women, with the long liripipe tail hanging down the back. By the end of the fourteenth century the noblewoman's hair was completely hidden by an increasingly important headdress, with a jewelled and embroidered caul, over which was attached an ornamental padded roll. Children in manuscript illustrations seem to wear chaperons, tunics and hoods, plainer replicas of their parents' clothes.

All this emphasis on the appearance of the clothing didn't hide the fact that people and their clothes must have smelt dreadful. In the fourteenth century not everyone washed, but they did use many scents and perfumes. Violet was most popular. Pomanders were made and a primitive atomizer, called a 'cyprus oyslet', sprinkled scented powder when it was squeezed. 'Hungarian water' was the first perfume with an alcohol base. It contained cedar, rosemary and turpentine and was given to Charles V of France in 1370. Smart women used creams and ointments, powders and toothpaste and dyed their hair blond or black, but never red which symbolized wickedness.

In the 1360s men were wearing an embarrassingly short, hip-length garment called the paltok, with their hose attached to the sides by laces with little metal tips, called points. The moralists were outraged, and blamed it on the foreigners, especially the fashionable Hainaulters who had arrived with Queen Philippa. Under the paltok, men wore a gibbon, also known as a pourpoint, jupon or jerkin, next to the shirt. It was tightly fitted and hooked at the sides, and was popular in its many variations, for over 100 years. It evolved from the gambeson, a thick, fur-lined or quilted garment worn to stop the armour from chaffing. By the second half of the fourteenth century it had become the doublet, with its two quilted layers. Ladies and hired needlewomen spent hours decorating surcoats, robes and mantles with heraldic devices. Style was everything. Sir John Chandos must have looked amazing as he took to the battlefield in 1370 under the command of the Black Prince. He might have escaped death, except he got tangled up in the folds of his lavish trailing embroidered robes.

After the French king John II, known as John the Good, died in 1364, men started to wear black as a sign of mourning and this convention continued, becoming even more severe for royal women. Eleanor of Pointiers, a court lady in the reign of Philip the Good, maintained that the Queen of France had to remain in her black-hung bedroom for a year, but less was demanded of other members of the court. The custom of wearing black probably came from Spain, but was not then a universally accepted colour for mourning. The Egyptians chose yellow, an allusion to withered leaves, the Ethiopians gray, a reminder of ashes, while white signified purity. After the period of mourning, deep violet could be worn, being a mixture of the red of royalty, and the blue of sorrow and trust in Heaven.

Of all the Kings of England, Richard II who reigned for 22 years from 1377 to 1399, was the most devoted to fashion and the butt of much criticism for his extravagance. Silk lampas and baldekyne were superseded by the fashionable satins and damasks and he had to be the first to have a black silk damask doublet. He adored velvet, and for his marriage to his second wife Isabella in 1396, he accumulated a splendid collection of figured velvets. They included polychrome or *mottele attabys,* voided velvet on a satin ground, *pann's'ici,* damask figured velvet, sometimes with gold, and even *velve velut,* an early reference to pile on pile velvet. He had one coat that was valued at 30,000 marks, and a long robe of green damask, made for his appearance in court in 1393-4. His uncle Thomas, Duke of Gloucester, also owned a gown and coat, (cloke) of black silk damask at the time of his disgrace in 1397. The dark coloured silks became a 'must have' fashion, but eventually Edward IV (1461-1483) limited its wear to people over the degree of knight, an edict clearly ignored by the people.

The Houppelande

By 1380 the cote-hardi was losing favour and men started to wear the houppelande, lined with fur for the winter. It was a loose, baggy, outer garment, flaring out from the padded shoulders, the first sign of the bulky look that would become such a distinctive feature in the Tudor age. The houppelande was full length but it got shorter over the next few decades, for all but the elderly. It had very full sleeves with a wide cuff. Soon an alternative, the bag sleeve, buttoned at the wrist became very popular because it could be a useful pocket or pouch. The neckline rose almost to the ears and was edged with fur. Its most distinctive feature was the pleats that formed

Lady wearing an elaborate stuffed horned headdress with a fur-edged super-tunic, now rather out of date, over a kirtle, her decorated girdle showing underneath, c1440s.

Smart young man wearing a short houppelande, split up the sides and lined with fur. Made of rich silks, it had bulky sleeves, a V-shaped neck, front and back and over his shoulder he carried a chapeau bras. He wore long pointed toed shoes. c1440

at the waist when it was belted. Initially the belt was placed at the natural waistline, but soon the fashion-conscious man wore his belt very low, on the hip. Over his shoulder he slung a hat, on a long ribbon. It was called a *chapeau bras* and was never intended to be actually worn on the head. Hose were often parti-coloured, one red and one green, cut on the cross. They had a seam up the back to improve the fit and were attached by points to the paltok. With them they wore long pointed shoes.

For some time, women had been wearing a vast circular floor-length cloak called a pelican or pelisson. It did not have defined sleeves, but otherwise was similar to the houppelande. The men's houppelande often opened down the front, but the women's was pulled on over the head. It was a very graceful garment, warm and comfortable, the distinctive radiating pleats held in place by a decorative belt placed just under the bust. The deep flowing sleeves could be a bit tricky to manage so it sometimes had decorated slits in the upper part of the sleeves for the arms to come through. These fitchets were edged with fur or braid, just like the old pelican cloak.

The high necks and collars required the hair to be drawn well off the face, and tucked under a headdress. Richard II's first wife, Anne of Bohemia, is credited with introducing some of the most extraordinary headpieces. By now the ear cauls or silk net crespines had crept higher, forming two little horns that would get progressively larger and wider. Some headdresses had a padded circular roll of fabric called a *bourrelet*, which gradually rose higher into a horseshoe shape, with a fitted decorated undercap underneath. Some had silk or linen veils, fluted and piled up and attached to wires or an under-prop. The men's hood changed shape, and instead of being worn like a balaclava, the whole chaperon was lifted up on top of the head. Sometimes the liripipe was flung nonchalantly over the shoulder, or pinned onto the costume, but more often the tail was wound around the chaperon on the head, holding it all in place and allowing the fancy dagged edges to show to advantage. Men of fashion soon got tired of doing this every time they put it on, so the tailor stitched it into place in the most flattering and becoming style adding feathers, fringes or garlands to give height and importance. To really put a price on your head, the feathers had to be ostrich, and they could be as valuable as the rest of the garments together.

Fifteenth Century Fashions

The early fifteenth century began with the reign of **Henry IV, (1399-1413). He was married to Mary Bohun in 1395 and later to Joan of Navarre. He was very sensitive about his right to kingship and cautious about spending too extravagantly or asking parliament for money. To keep down the cost on his cloth of gold or velvet, he sometimes had the weft made of yellow silk. The long enveloping fur-lined heugue became popular, possibly as an antidote to the short tunics and houppelandes, which rose higher and higher. The hose also crept upward over the thighs until eventually, in a stroke of genius they were joined together as tights and combined with the breeches. Some hose were soled with soft leather, and wooden pattens or clogs were worn over them in wet weather.**

This lady is wearing a pelisson over her tight sleeved and buttoned surcoat. The couvre-chef and wimple indicate she is a married woman.

The whole silhouette for women was tall and willowy and by the mid-fifteenth century had reached its apogee. The long trained gowns, with the high tight belt, decorated with jewels for special occasions, drew attention to the tiny bust. The neckline of the gown became wider, forming a deep V in the centre front and the outer edges rolled over to form a collar making a splendid area for the display of beautiful jewellery. The wide sleeves got longer and trailed on the ground, while the silk damask undergown's tight sleeves covered the knuckles. Headdresses came in a wide variety of shapes: turbans, truncated flower pots, horned, triangular, fluted, or suspended on wires like fluttering butterflies. The hennin or steeple headdress caused a sensation with its long diaphanous silk veil that allowed the beautiful silk damask cone to show through. It was fashionable at the Burgundian court, though less often seen in England. Most headdresses had a little velvet loop in the centre front, to help adjust and pull the headdress into place. They all had one thing in common: not a single hair was permitted to show. The high smooth forehead gave the high-browed look and any offending hair had to be plucked out.

Not everyone was the fashionable shape and women started wearing a short-sleeved corselet, laced in front with a wire belt to tighten the waist and push up the bust. Some women inserted little pads into their chemise to improve the bustline and a pad was placed on the stomach under the gown to give the stylish full rounded line, a fashion credited to Isabeau of Bavaria who was rather plump.

Tightly buttoned long sleeves cover the knuckles, high belt emphasising a small bust, fur on collar and hem. The butterfly headdress is wired to hold the silk veiling, while the richly embossed net crespine and band cover the ears and forehead. c1465

Her shape just wasn't right for the current look, and she went to endless trouble, taking baths in asses' milk, sweating for hours in steam rooms, having the physician place cupping glasses all over her body, all in the pursuit of fashion. Naturally she had a whole range of cosmetics at hand, made up of crocodile glands, boars' brains and wolves' blood, combined with strange oils.

As the women's clothes got longer and more extravagant, the men's got shorter and shorter, the doublets were boned and stiffened. By now the long-toed shoes had become absurd, and rumour has it that the points had to be stuffed with tow or moss or held up by a little chain attached to a band under the knee. It was all rather extreme. Then quite suddenly the fashion for the high headdress was over. The hennin was shortened and set at the back of the head, still with its velvet loop but now with a small transparent silk veil, folded in the centre to give a heart shape. A black gauze hood with a veil was introduced, which fell onto the shoulders and later developed into the French hood of the sixteenth century. Collars got flatter and spread out on the shoulders away from the V-shaped neck. The wide sleeves were slashed to show the rich brocaded undersleeve, or the fine pleated lawn chemise. It is said that slashing the fabric started in Germany, but by 1450 it had spread to France and England. The *Roman de la Rose* mentions 'sewn in sleeves', a reference to the practice of varying the costume by having extra sets of sleeves, made of rich fabric and laced onto the garment. The *surcotes ouvertes* or front-opening women's gown heralded a further change. The stiffened farthingale or 'keep thy virtue' was initially a highly decorated V-shaped section of petticoat, starched and covered with taffeta. It was said to have been invented in 1470 by the wife of King Henry V of Portugal, who tried to hide her illicit pregnancy from her impotent husband. Some gowns had a decorative hem that could be replaced when it got worn or irretrievably dirty. The whole shape of women's dress was changing, becoming wider on the shoulders, and more cone-shaped and structured in the skirt, with wide split sleeves gathered into the wrist with voluminous outer sleeves, and lacy frills. Some immense oversleeves were turned back and edged with fur – a last reminder of the Middle Ages and heralding the bulky square look of the Tudor period.

Practical:
Handspinning Silk

A young spinner, her overtunic tucked up like an apron.
From a drawing by Jean Fouquet probably before 1460.

Spinning Silk

Silk is a joy and a delight, and working with it can change your life. There are many different styles of silk fibre and ways to spin it, so choose the silk and the method that produces the perfect thread for your project.

There is no wrong way to spin silk, but most problems arise from thinking that all silks are the same and there is only one way to spin it; into a long smooth glossy thread, as finely as possible. Some silks, like top quality Bombyx mori and tussah silks can be spun this way, but many of the other styles have short fibres, are knotty, chalky in colour or sticky to handle and make wonderful novelty yarns. Many people learn to spin wool first, where the finest, thinnest yarn is the most highly esteemed, but silk is silk, not wool, and should be handled in different ways. If silk is thinly spun like superfine wool, it will look and feel like string. It will drop and lose its sparkle and lustrous feel, the very things that make silk special.

Wool has more bounce than silk. To compensate for this lack of elasticity, silk should be spun in such a way as to trap air in with the fibres. The main object in spinning silk is to spin fibre around air. This is done by first spinning the silk quite softly to incorporate the most air and then plying it more firmly to make a soft, rounded yarn. If the reverse is done, with a tightly spun and loosely plied yarn, the result is a hard, dull, stringy thread with the light and life squeezed out of it.

Butterfly Jacket, with soft, rainbow colours and butterflies fair-isled down the back. Handspun pure silk, hand dyed and knitted.

Preparing your wheel

Start by oiling your wheel. Silk is very light and if you have been using your wheel for greasy wool, you will need to clean and oil the moving parts to make them run smoothly and to ensure that the silk remains clean.

Follow the manufacturer's instructions and oil your wheel in a methodical way, so no part is missed; across the top, then the middle section, and finally across the bottom. Put the tiniest drop of oil on the leathers, along the spindle shaft, around the orifice, and on either side of the bobbin. Now apply a drop of oil to each point across the middle section of your wheel, including the centre hole, and finally around the foot peddles. Sit comfortably, and quietly treadle using both feet. Establish a gentle continuous rhythm, to distribute the oil evenly.

Almost all wheels will accommodate two feet, even if the treadle is very small. Lucky you if you have a double treadle! Try this experiment: treadle using one foot, and feel the angle of your back. It will twist and sag lower on one side. If you doubt this, sit in front of a mirror. Now place two feet on the treadle, and note how you are sitting more squarely on the chair, and your back has become balanced. If you want to spin for hours at a time, and your back to last in good condition until the end of your life, you need to learn to treadle with two feet. It will feel a bit odd to begin with, but persevere. It is like learning any new skill, and once you feel that sense of balance, you will be pleased to have made the change.

From the top:
Botswanan silk
Tussah silk
Bombyx mori

Spinning Silk

There are many different styles and forms of silk suitable for spinning, but the two most readily available are the domesticated white Bombyx mori and the wild, honey-coloured tussah. They both come in a myriad of different grades. Start with an A1 grade silk brick, tops or sliver, the best you can find. Do not be tempted to think that any silk, because it is called silk, will do. It is too hard to spin a beautiful, smooth, lustrous thread using scrappy, dull, poor quality silk.

To prepare the silk for spinning, first check the quality and length of the staple, because that will determine the way you spin it. Carefully tear off a 20cm (8 inch) portion of silk fibre. Grasp one end of the silk and fold the fingers over it, against the palm of the hand, to anchor it. Use the thumb and first finger of the other hand like a gentle clamp, about 5cm (2 inches) lower. Hear the silk click and make a snapping sound as you give it a little pull. Keep moving the bottom hand down the silk, a little at a time until the fibres start to part. Notice the gloss, and the way good quality silk will have all the fibres lying parallel and open, free of knots, noils and tangles. Good spinning silk should have a staple length of between 8-15 cm, (3-6 inches). It could be a mixture of lengths, so check it to find the average. If the silk is very short in the staple, matted, dull or a poor colour, set it aside for another project and find some better quality silk. There are other methods for spinning short staple silk; nothing is wasted.

Take the primary thread on your bobbin, and pass it through the front orifice on your wheel. Hold it firmly in either hand, whichever one is right for you. Turn the wheel clockwise and gently start treadling. Use the thumb and first finger to pinch and slide down the primary thread, controlling the position of the twist.

Now take a 20cm (8 inch) length of silk and flick the furry ends underneath the primary thread between the orifice and your fingers, so that the silk fibres are gathered in by the twisting primary thread. Keep the thumb and first finger of the front hand always on the thread, controlling the position of the twist, as you gently slide your fingers down the silk, smoothing it as you go. The back hand has an equally important but different job to do. It must prepare the silk to be spun by fanning it out over the palm of your front hand. The fanned out fibres make a wide V, and it is easy to glance down and check that all the fibres are lying smoothly and are incorporating as much air as possible. That is the secret: the back hand must keep preparing the silk by fanning it out. Do not be tempted to dampen your fingers to help to twist and roll the threads, as you would with linen. Silk absorbs any trace of dust and grime, especially when it is damp. This will show up as grey streaks in the knitting and weaving, and will not come out later, despite careful washing. Lines of discoloured silk can look most unsightly and spoil the whole effect.

Joining in the furry ends for Bombyx mori and Tussah silk.

Fanning out the silk and working it over the palm of the hand

Photos: Chris Moltzer

The two most important things are:

- The front hand must squeeze and slide down the fibre controlling the position of the twist and smoothing the thread, never jumping on and off, unless you want lumps and slubs.

- The back hand must prepare the silk fibre, opening it by fanning it out, and working in rhythm to let the spun silk gather onto the bobbin.

Things to check

The tension should be balanced, neither so tight that it grabs and drags the spun fibre onto the bobbin, nor so loose that the thread sags and is not taken up. The wheel must play its part, and draw the thread smoothly and firmly onto the bobbin. If the thread dips as it goes towards the orifice, adjust the tension knob, a fraction at a time. Keep tightening the tension until the balance feels just right, and you can feel the wheel drawing the silk smoothly onto the bobbin.

Some silk, especially tussah, may 'fly' when you start opening it up and spinning it. Try folding the length of sliver in half, so there is a smooth loop of silk at the bottom, and double the amount of fluffy ends to join in. This smooth loop is much less liable to break up and 'fly' as it rubs against your knees. If the fibre gets matted and muddled in your hands, try folding it over the first finger and spinning from the fold.

Check the height of your chair to ensure that it is neither too high nor too low and sit well back in a relaxed position. If you crouch forward over your work, your back will ache. This is a long, smooth drawing system, and your nose does not have to be involved. A short, jerky spin, poking and pushing the silk onto the bobbin, can be very slow and tiring. Consciously relax your hands to ensure a soft spin. Good quality silk has a long fibre and won't escape, so there is no need to grip it tightly. Keep your hands a good distance apart to lengthen the draw, and let the wheel do most of the work. The longer and smoother the draw, the more even the twist and the faster the silk will be spun onto the bobbin.

Always work the silk fibre over the open palm of your front hand, so a quick glance at any time will allow you to see the state of the fibre as it is incorporated, thin it out, remove lumps and prepare

Sit back in a relaxed position and keep your hands a good distance apart as you fan out the silk

the right amount of silk for this particular yarn. This is very important if you plan to read while you spin. Just prop your book up - your hands can feel what to do, it is that easy.

Spinning sets up its own rhythm and if you are peddling quietly, then your thoughts and hands will move together. The silk will work its own magic and a feeling of contentment, harmony and balance will result. Your heart rate will slow down and you will have a sense of well-being, a time out, a real bonus in a busy life. When you sit at your wheel, you are part of a harmonious circle that joins your feet with your back, your head, heart, hands, the silk and the wheel. Choose your favourite music, possibly Mozart or Vivaldi, but perhaps not the William Tell overture, which could have you galloping along!

If silk spinning is new to you, undoubtedly the hardest part will be to make a thread thick and even enough to knit, crochet, or use as a weft for weaving. Alternatively, you may want your silk to be very thin and tightly spun for a warp, embroidery or lacemaking. You can determine exactly the character of the yarn for your project. An expert is not the person who can spin the finest, thinnest thread but the one who can spin beautifully, all weights and styles. The experienced spinner chooses different silks and appropriate methods for different projects. If you want the longest, finest silk, say for a warp, there is an argument for buying it ready spun on a cone and spinning a silk yarn with more character for the weft. If you spin the silk in ways that the manufacturer cannot, your work will be fresh and unique, a reflection of your individuality and talent.

Try this experiment. Spin up the first section on your bobbin, and then as you change to the next hook, consciously try to spin the next section a little thicker, and so on, as you move over the hooks. Do the same with the next bobbin, so that when you come to ply it, you can actually see and feel the difference. Every so often, double the spun thread back on itself to gauge the way it will look and feel once it is plied. If you want to knit using commercial patterns, your silk needs to be comparable to a four-ply or double knitting yarn. Silk also needs to be knitted on at least one size smaller needles than wool of the same weight. Test it, by knitting a sample of your plied silk, and see if you like the results. You can choose to spin the thickness you want. Start spinning and see how it goes.

Bombyx mori jacket trimmed with dark tussah silk.
See detail below.
Photos: Bill Wilson

Plying Silk

With plying, if your wheel allows it, put the driving band on a size smaller whorl to put more twist in the thread and improve the ratio. Place both full bobbins on your lazy kate, slightly behind your chair, so you have a nice long draw, with the thread on both bobbins parallel and at the same tension. If it is hard to get a long draw because your bobbins are on pins on the wheel itself, try threading the bobbins on two knitting needles suspended in a shoe box.

The trick with plying silk is to ensure that both threads keep an equal tension and one thread is not joining in at a looser tension or worse, wrapping itself around the other thread. This uneven tension may not be obvious at first, but when you come to knit it, the garment will have a diagonal pull, the stitches all marching resolutely off to one side. Knitting a sample will reveal this straight away. Unfortunately this yarn will not come right, even after washing, stretching, weighting or blocking.

Back to plying: attach your two threads to the primary thread on the bobbin on your wheel. There are lots of methods, but a reef knot (right over left and under, left over right and under) is an excellent choice because it will just pull apart smoothly when you are finished. Place the fingers of your front hand between the threads, to control each separately, and pinch them to control the position of the twist.

Place the fingers of your other hand well behind you, separating the threads and pinching and controlling them. Keep each thread under equal tension. Treadle, turning the wheel in the opposite direction, probably anti-clockwise if you have spun your silk clockwise in the first instance. Now check the tension on your wheel. It will probably have to be tightened a bit, as it should feel as if the threads are being quite firmly drawn onto the bobbin. Continue treadling smoothly until all the silk has been plied. Try counting, "one-two-let it on", to establish an easy rhythm with a regular number of treadles and twists.

Black and white houndstooth jacket. Handspun and knitted Bombyx mori and black wool. See detail below

Washing Silk

The plied silk needs to be skeined and washed to allow it to settle and to set the twist. This step is essential with silk, as unwashed and untextured silk can drop up to four inches over the length of a knitted back or sleeve. Loosely tie the skeins in four places and then fill a bowl with hand-hot water. Add your usual hand-washing liquid, a silk wash like Tenestar, or even a good quality dishwashing liquid with a neutral Ph rating. Avoid soap powder. If the powder does not dissolve completely it will leave specks on the silk, and most machine washing powders are too harsh. They contain additives and whiteners to bleach and remove difficult stains and are not suitable for silk.

Handspun, knitted and dyed pure silk patchwork jacket.
See detail below

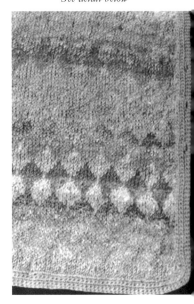

Slosh the skeins gently up and down so they get completely wet, but do not leave them to soak. Squeeze the water out and refill the bowl. Rinse the silk twice more with warm water, of the same or slightly cooler temperature, to rinse the silk completely. You may wish to use a little water softener or fabric conditioner, add a drop of vinegar, or baby oil. We all have our favourite methods, dependent on the quality of the local water supply. Squeeze the water out of the skeins and roll them in a towel and stamp on them. This is much better than twisting them. If you have a number of skeins, then put them in a wash bag and spin the water out using a medium fast spin and the final 'spin only' setting on your washing machine.

The silk skeins will look just awful, dull and nasty, but do not despair. Give each skein a really good shake and hang it on an airing frame, or on the line but not in the bright sun. Every time you go past, give it a shake, to allow the air back into the fibres and to break them up so they don't cling together looking flat and miserable. Finally, when the skeins are almost dry, put them in the tumble-dryer on a medium heat for a few minutes to fluff them up, or give them a really good beating by flicking them against the back of a chair and snapping them between your hands. An excellent exercise for a bad day. Silk is tough and strong, and will come up smiling, its lustre and softness restored. You are in charge so do not be afraid of it.

Waterfall jacket, handspun and knitted from Bombyx mori pure silk, dyed in cascading shades from greens, blues and into touches of cerise – see detail below

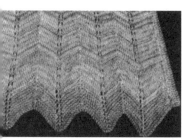

Different Styles of silks

Silk comes in lots of different forms as well as bricks, slivers and tops. All spinning silks are 'waste silk'. This is rather a misnomer as all silks are useful. 'Waste silk' refers to all the different styles of silk fibre except filament silk, the continuous thread that has been wound off the cocoon.

Most varieties of silk come in both Bombyx mori and various shades of tussah, as well as being bleached, carded or combed. Some you might find are:

· Silk bricks, both Bombyx mori and Tussah
· Carded, combed silks, sliver and tops
· Floss, Blaze and Cocoon strippings
· Bleached or carded silk noils
· Degummed cocoons
· Mawata caps and handkerchiefs
· Throwsters silk, both white and multicoloured
· Laps and batts
· Gummy silk
· Carrier rod waste

The biggest mistake is to try to spin them all into a long, smooth, glossy thread. They are not all designed to do that. You choose the method of spinning to match the fibre, to produce a particular result. As all silk is imported, mostly from China, the different forms of silk are not always available. If you find a special one, get enough to complete your project.

Silk Bricks. These are made up of thick, untwisted ropes of silk fibres, carded and finely combed, about 3 metres long and weighing between 125 and 150 grams. Each is wound into a brick shape and usually packed into lots of 16 bricks, about 2 kilograms in total weight. The bricks can vary considerably in quality. The best is A1. These are fully carded and finely combed, bright and glossy, with fine even fibres around 10-15cm (4-6 inches) in length, free of knots and rubbish. Choose a long smooth spinning method, for a glorious lustrous top quality yarn. Lesser quality bricks can be duller and more chalky, more matted in texture, carded but not combed, with a staple length of as little as 2cm, (1 inch) so beware! Always check the staple length, or ask for a sample before you buy.

Carded and combed silks. These are mixed length fibres, which may have been carded and/or combed, and are usually sold as sliver, rovings or tops. They come in various qualities so do check the fibre length, colour and the texture before buying. With care, they can spin up nicely into a smooth yarn using a woollen spin, but the yarn is usually less lustrous or more chalky and may not be A1 quality. Some are described as cut silk, and some have a very short staple. Both these sorts spin into a wonderful, soft, slubby yarn. This can be a good silk to hand-card with other fibres, and is the usual way of presenting mixed fibres, silk carded with wool, alpaca, cotton, linen etc.

Laying the primary thread over the cocoon strippings

Blaze, Floss and Cocoons strippings. These silks are the short, broken fibres from the outside of the cocoon and the last weak fibres inside the cocoon, before and after the filament thread is reeled off. They come in a variety of natural colours from white to dark brown, including a super egg-yoke yellow. The yellow is in the sericin gum, and will wash out eventually with repeated hot washings. The fibre has a matt finish and the texture is usually more like cotton. Blaze is the loose silk the silkworm has spun to attach itself to the twigs or frame before starting to spin the actual cocoon. Silk floss has traditionally been used for embroidery. Cocoon strippings that have been partly degummed can be used in felt and paper making. Degummed cocoon strippings are very easy to spin. Check the staple length and if it is over 2cm or 1 inch, then use a woollen spin. If it is much shorter, then take a handful of the silk strippings and lie the primary thread across it. Watch the twist pick up the short fibres and draw them into a thread. This is similar to a cotton spin. The finger and thumb of the front hand pinch and release the twist to let it run into the mass of the silk. Keep drawing out your back hand, until your arm is fully extended, then let the thread wind firmly onto the bobbin. Experiment with the tension, until you get the wheel doing half the work of drawing out the strippings and then springing the spun thread back onto the bobbin. It's a balancing act.

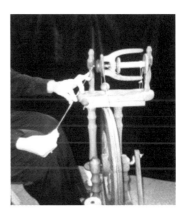

Pinch and relax the front hand to release the twist, while drawing the back hand further and further back.

Noil, uncarded, carded and bleached. Noil has great possibilities. It has the shortest fibre length of all the waste silks and some noil is little better than floor sweepings. Noils are the little knots and knops, the residue left after the silk has been repeatedly carded, combed and the best silk removed. The fibres often contain little bits of rubbish, including the last skin shed by the silkworm, which shows up as black flecks. Uncarded noil is just a mass of knots and bits, and needs to be carded. It rarely has a staple length of more than 0.5cm and has little gloss, but takes the dye very well. Unwashed noil can be filthy, but washed and carded noil makes an interesting textured, high twist yarn. Carded noil can also come as fragile sheetings with a pleated effect, the result of going through the carding machine. Try rolling small sections into a soft cylinder and holding it right inside your back hand. Lay the primary thread through the middle of it, and let the twist come right down and inside the cylinder of silk, gathering the very short fibres into itself. This can be done with one hand only, or use the top/front hand to pinch and release to control the amount of twist, and ease out any thicker parts that form in the thread. This high twist, low lustre thread dyes beautifully, and is excellent for giving texture to weaving or for plying with other more slippery silks.

Degummed Cocoons. This is the innermost part of the cocoon, after the pupa has been extracted. The fibres have been washed and dried, to remove the gum. They are of mixed length, some very long indeed, and are mixed in with the mass of little bobbles. You could tease the bobbles out and spin the silk as usual, but why would you, when it spins into a fantastic, bobbly thread. Tighten the tension a little on your wheel and tear off a handful of the degummed cocoons. It is not necessary to open it all out, unless you are trying to make a long smooth thread. Use its intrinsic character and let the bobbles spin through, like beads on a string. This silk has a wonderful texture and looks fantastic when incorporated into a woven piece, or as part of a fancy pattern in a knitted garment.

Mawata Caps and Handkerchiefs. Mawata is made from the broken cocoons where the silkmoth has emerged. The cocoons now have a hole at one end, so it is no longer possible to unwind it as a continuous filament. The sericin or silk gum is dissolved in hot water, and then the cocoons are stretched out over a porcelain cap-shaped frame, one layer on top of another, something between 8 and 15 layers of separate cocoons to form a 'cap'. A bundle of around 30 caps is called a 'bell.'

There is a 'Proper Way', and an 'Easy Way' to deal with mawata. The Proper Way is to punch a hole through the cap, and stretch it out into an ever larger circle, which gets thinner and longer until it eventually breaks forming a long length. This is altogether far too difficult as the fibres stick together. It is hard on your hands, hard

Separating a Mawata cap

on your shoulders, and hard to spin and control the thickness. There is an Easy Way to deal with mawata caps. Put one hand right up inside the cap, and grab almost all the other layers except the top one, which you pinch with your outside hand. With a quick snap, pull your hands apart, and one complete layer comes off. Even better, it is already in a large V shape, allowing plenty of air around the fibres so they do not stick together. It requires no further preparation and is ready to spin on your wheel, spindle or thigh roll. It is quick, easy and not tiring at all. With the handkerchiefs, just peel off one layer at a time. Both caps and handkerchiefs dye beautifully, and as the colour goes right through, the rainbow effect can be magical.

Joining in throwsters waste

Throwsters silk. This silk comes from the waste from the throwing and twisting machines. Sometimes throwsters waste is made up of warp ends, cut off the loom after the weaving has been completed. It comes as a mass of glossy, crimpy fibres and spins up into an exciting imitation boucle. Start by roughly cutting the tangled mass into 5-13cm (2-5 inch) lengths. It will not work unless the fibres are cut up. Put it on a tray on your lap, because it goes everywhere. After tightening the tension on the breaking band on your wheel, join in the chopped up throwsters silk, letting the loose, springy fibres spin together. Work really quickly, taking no care at all to make it smooth and even, which would defeat the purpose. The shorter the lengths, the more boucle the effect, and the more firmly it needs to be spun. Throwsters silk is slippery, so ply it quite firmly with a rough, sticky silk like mawata or a hand or commercially spun noil. It will catch on the hooks of the flyer, so hook it around only the first and last hooks, running along the backs of the others, so it does not catch so easily. Throwsters silk adds a super texture to both knitting and weaving, dyes like a dream and is great fun to do.

Laps and batts. These sheets of silks are made from poor quality silk laid out into a thick airy layer. They can be split through the middle, handspun, and have an interesting crepe bandage texture. They can be used for patchwork or filling quilts or jackets, dyed, used for felt and paper making or incorporated into embroidery or other crafts.

Gummy silk. This silk is so named because the sericin has not been washed out of it. The threads are strong and springy, like horsehair and the long length means that the fibres can be threaded through a needle for embroidery. Also, the gum makes this silk ideal for incorporating in felt and paper making.

Carrier Rod Waste. This is not a silk fibre as such. It is formed from the fine silk strands that got caught up around the carrier rods which carry the silk filament from the cocoon as it unwinds onto the reels. Every so often it must be cut off, and these little hard lengths of matted silk, about 15 x 2cm (6 x 1 inch) are collected up. Although they can smell terrible, this goes after they have been soaked briefly. The water softens them and they become pliable, and the layers peel off, like crepe bandage. They take the dye well, and are perfect for imaginative uses in embroidery or incorporating into felt or paper.

There is no limit to the uses of the different silks, so explore and experiment.

Appendix

The Silk Routes across Asia

Traders and travellers left the large vibrant Chinese city of Ch'ang-an (Xi'an) by the West Gate, and travelled over 250 miles, following the Great Wall up the windswept Wei Valley, with its mulberry trees ringing the paddy fields, up what came to be known as the Imperial Highway. The route followed the Huang, the Yellow River, which springs from the K'unlun Mountains, and the Nan Shan or Southern Mountains along the Kansu Corridor. It skirted the dry expanse of the Gobi Desert by way of Wuwei, Zhangyi, Jiayuquan, and Anxi to Dunhuang, near the Caves of the Thousand Buddhas. It took the Polos 40 days to cross the Gobi Desert in the thirteenth century, compared with two and a half days now, by train.

Leaving Dunhuang, there was a choice of two or three trading routes. The T'ien Shan Nan Lu, or the 'Road South of the Celestial Mountains', begins at the Yumen Kuan or Jade Gate. It goes westwards towards Loulan, skirting the northern edge of the Tarim Basin via the salt-encrusted Lop Desert. Loulan was once an important city, but by the third century the rivers had dried up, making travelling almost impossible. The road proceeded through Karashahr (Yanqi), Kucha, (Kuga) Aksu and Kashgar (Kashi), then crossed the treacherous Pamir Mountains to reach Ferghana, known for its splendid horses, fed on the rich alfalfa. This part of the road, called the Royal or Golden Road to Samarkand, continued towards the Iranian Plateau, passing the cities of Samarkand and Bukhara. Both cities had bazaars and caravanserai and were heavily fortified. The route continued to Persia, re-joining the road to Antioch and the Mediterranean at Merv (Mary).

The most northern route left the road at Anhsi, 90 miles east of Dunhuang and crossed parts of the Gobi Desert, to Hami, famous for its melons, dried raisins and sweet wine. The city of Turfan lies 300 feet below sea level, resulting in extreme temperatures; 40 degrees Centigrade below in winter and 40 degrees above in summer. The route continued alongside the snowcapped peaks of the T'ien Shan or Celestial Mountains to Beshbalik and Almalik, across the semi-arid Dzungarian Basin to Altai and the Golden Mountains, past the warm salt lake, Issyk Kul, to Tashkent and Samarkand. This route was called the T'ien Shan Pei Lu, the 'Road North of the Celestial Mountains'. It was the easiest route during the Tang and Mongol Dynasties, but as there was seldom peace, it offered easy pickings for bandits.

The southern route was difficult because there were fewer oases where travellers could rest and replenish their provisions, but they were also less likely to be attacked by marauders. The traveller left by the Yang Kuan Gate, going south-west following the 'Road North of the Southern Mountain'. The route skirts the vast Taklamakan Desert, 600 miles across by 250 north to south, through Cherchen avoiding the bleak and hostile salt desert around Lop Nor. It crossed the kingdoms of Niya, Wumi, Pishan and Khotan (Hotan), a city renowned for its carpets, taffetas, felts, silks and the finest white and green jade. The route gradually rose towards Yarkand and on to Kashgar (Kashi), 5000 feet above sea level, with its famous Sunday Market, bazaars and orchards. It entered the Karakorum Range, the Tsung-ling or Onion Mountains and the High Pamirs. People believed that it was the wild onions that made them feel ill, but it was really the high altitude and thin air. Hou Han Shu, in 96 AD, wrote feelingly of places like Little Headache, Great Headache and Land of Fever. The route emerged onto the high plateaus, where there was good water and grazing. It was easier now, following the wide river valleys between the Oxus ie the Amu Darya and the Jaxartes or Syr Darya into Western Turkestan, Uzbekistan, Kazakhstan and parts of Afghanistan. Balkh was the half way point, the crossroad city of the routes to India and the Mediterranean.

The route continued to Balkh, Merv (Mary), Ectbatana, Ctesiphon and Palmyra to the Mediterranean Sea. Some travellers went from Merv to Rayy and Alamut, which was near the modern city of Qazuin. It was the base of the Sh'ia sect called the Assassins, led by the Old Man of the Mountains. This route went on to Ecbatana and Hamadan, to the Zagros Mountains and the Mesopotamian cities of Babylon, Selecia, Ctesaphon and Baghdad. The route to India went via the Hindu Kush, following the Indus River in Pakistan on the border of Afghanistan and Kashmir, to the Persian Gulf where the goods were loaded into ships sailing to western countries. The Iranian Plateau was often avoided because of the exorbitant taxes and bribes, so merchants went further north to Baku and the Black Sea.

Travellers on the Great Desert Route used two humped Bactrian camels that could carry up to 500 pounds each. The camels walked at a steady three miles per hour, the camel master in absolute control. There are tales of blind camel masters, whose profound knowledge of the route enabled them to sense the right direction and find water from the smell and direction of the wind. Asses, donkeys, yaks and horses were also used, depending on the terrain and climate. Often the caravan travelled at night guided by the stars, to avoid bandits and the blistering heat. Large caravans of several hundred people could take as long as eight or nine years to travel from Ch'ang-an to Persia or northern India and back.

Another branch of the route went to Aleppo and Antioch and into Syria, travelling down the river to the Persian Gulf, to Palmyra the city of Palms, or via Babylon, to Petra, Gaza, Alexandria, and the Phoenican cities of Tyre, Sidon and Byblos. Sometimes the choice was to by-pass the cities, and head for the Aegean Sea and Miletus, Ephesus, Smyna and Troy to Trebizon and Byzantium.

The Northern Route via the Eurasian Steppes went north of the Aural, Caspian and Black Seas, to the Plains of Poland and Germany or south to the Danube Valley into the heart of Europe. It was the easier route with vast plains, fewer mountains, no deserts or harsh climate. It was ideal for wheeled carts, but also for fast marauding nomads.

Medieval Silk Vestments and Secular Embroidered Items

Medieval ecclesiastical embroideries use symbols as secret signs to tell stories to the faithful. The fish, which was the pagan symbol of life, was a reminder that Christ was a fisherman, a fisher of men. The Chi Rho is the earliest monogram of Christ in both the eastern and western church and was adopted by Constantine in 313 AD. The IHS gradually replaced the Chi Rho. The Tau cross was disguised to form the mast and rigging of a ship and has connections with sun worship, a reminder of the scroll inscription nailed above the crucifixion cross.

The triangle or three interconnecting circles were symbols of the trinity. The star is a double triangle, the seal of Solomon, perfect god and perfect man, soul and body meeting at the apex and pointing upward to God. Paintings and embroideries show the hand of God coming down in a blaze of light, or tongues of flame to symbolise Pentecost, or dove the symbol for the Holy Spirit.

Symbols of the Passion and crucifixion include ladders, dice, nails, pinchers, sponge, sword, spear, bag with silver coins, rope, drops of blood, whip, crown of thorns and a book to foretell what was to come. There are depictions of the Virgin Mary knitting a jersey, a reminder of the coat that the soldiers drew lots for, because it could not be torn and divided.

The pilgrims who went to the holy site of St James of Compostella wore a scallop shell in their caps. There are easily recognisable symbols for the four evangelists, Mathew the angel, Luke the bull, John the eagle and Mark the lion, while the shepherds at Bethlehem tend their sheep, the pascal lamb, the opus dei of St John the Baptist. A vast range of flowers had special significance.

Most of the saints and martyrs had their own symbols, often a reminder of how they died for the faith. There are the keys of St Peter, the sword of St Paul, the diagonal cross of St Andrew, St Mary Magdalene's jar of ointment and St Margaret's dragon. St Barbara has a tower and St Lucy her eyes, St Catherine her wheel or a sword and St Dorothy a basket of flowers. St Lawrence had his grill-iron, St Bartholemew his flaying knife, St Stephen some stones and St Sebastian his arrows. Other martyrs carry a palm leaf.

A great number of symbols are associated with the Virgin Mary. She has the five pointed Star of Bethlehem, her initials VM, AM for Ave Maria, crowned M and the typically English symbol of the mythical unicorn. She wears a halo, is often dressed in a blue robe, and a lily is included in any annunciation scene. The rose and the crescent moon, the symbol of Byzantium, is also a reminder of the feminine principle. Mary is depicted standing on the crescent moon, in the John of Thanet embroidered panel in the V&A. The sun and moon rising refers to Revelations 12, with stars guiding providence.

Alb	Evolved from the loose Roman under-tunic and worn under the chasuble by all the clergy. Before 1200 it was mostly made of linen, occasionally coloured silk, cloth of gold or velvet. Gradually the shape became simpler, and the sleeves tighter. Albs were decorated with embroidered patches called apparels.
Amice	A separate collar worn under the alb. It evolved from a hood, and was made of plain fabric, with an ornamental strip along the top edge.
Alms purse	Worn hanging from the belt and made of embroidered silk or rich fabric cut from other items. It was a medieval expectation that all wealthy or noble people gave alms to the poor.
Altar Frontal	Decorative silk textile made to hang in front of the altar. The Nevill Frontal of 1523 has embroidered items appliqued to the stamped silk velvet. Ralph Nevill was the 4th Earl of Westmoreland and his seven sons kneel on one side facing his wife Lady Catherine Swafford and her thirteen daughters. Red silk velvet was replaced in 17th century.
Apparels	Patches of rich silk or embroidered fabric sewn onto the alb, one each on the front and back near the hem, two on the chest and back, one on each cuff, and sometimes one around the neckline, covered by the amice. Apparels could also be made from older used vestments, like Thomas Becket's at Christ Church Canterbury. One embroidered set of apparels at the V&A has scenes from the Life of the Virgin, including the Hand of God.
Banners, Battle Standards and Pennons	An important item of rituals in church, guilds and war, often dedicated to a patron saint. One richly embroidered banner used by King Alfred (871-900), was reputedly the work of a Danish princess. Another one dated 1556-58 is red silk damask woven in a pattern of curvi-linear lattice of stems and foliage, painted in gold, black and a little blue, with the Trinity, the Assumption of the Virgin and John the Baptist and with figures of the evangelists in the corner.
Buskins, gaiters and silk cloth stockings	Tied with ribbons and worn by bishops. Stockings are not mentioned until the twelfth century when they are referred to by Ivo of Chartres and Honorius of Autun. Fragments of a set of buskins were found in a tomb in Worcester Cathedral believed to be that of Walter de Cantelupe, Bishop of Worcester (1236-66). These were made of brownish red silk twill, with silver-gilt thread embroidered with underside couching.

Chasuble	Developed from the Roman overcoat, paenula or casula and worn by the priest during the mass, and on special occasions by deacons, sub-deacons and abbots. It was originally circular but changed to fiddle or shield shape because of the difficulty in raising the arms when elevating the host. It was made of silk or fine wool with an added embroidered centre band, called an orphrey. Only Cathedrals could afford chasubles in a range of liturgical colours. Salisbury in the early thirteenth century had three sets, some old and worn, as did Norfolk in 1368. The Clare Chasuble (1272-94) was carefully embroidered in silk and gilt on navy silk twill. Around 130 years later with a change of fashion and need for speed, the Erphingham Chasuble was made of rich imported silk and gold damask with mass-produced embroidered slips of saints edged with braid to form the orphrey.
Chimerie	Sleeveless outer garment worn open at the front by bishops and archbishops, in black or scarlet, or by clergy with a doctor's degree.
Cope	Cope is derived from the 'lacerna', a semi-circular mantle, originally worn by officers in the Roman army. By the seventh century it developed into an ecclesiastical garment, at first used outdoors on processional occasions. The cope became the principal vestment of officiating priests and assistant clergy at the Mass. Silk coppae are first mentioned in an eighth century Spanish inventory, becoming ever more richly decorated and embroidered. The fragmented Butler-Bowden cope (1330-40) has always been in the family's possession and was reassembled in the nineteenth century onto red silk velvet. The Syon cope (1300-20) has been lovingly protected and preserved, the green and gold silk floss embroidery still in perfect condition.
Dalmatic	Similar in shape to an alb but shorter with square cut sleeves, made of rich fabric and worn by a deacon, sometimes by a bishop, over an alb. It followed the colours of the chasuble and by the fourteenth century had become more ornate with splits up the sides, bordered with a different colour or fabric and often paired with a tunicle. The highly decorated dark blue and gold dalmatic mentioned in the 1315-16 inventory of Canterbury, formerly belonged to Archbishop Lanfranc.
Dorsal/dossal	Rich curtain, often silk, hanging behind the altar. Dorsals were sometimes made from royal garments, given as gifts to churches, and re-cut to make vestments and furnishings.
Frontlet/Superfrontal	Narrow band decorating the top of the altar frontal. The only known signed piece of Opus Anglicanum is an altar frontal dated 1290-1340 at the V&A. It has a white ground with a row of gold

quatrefoils, each containing one letter of an inscription. The words DOMNA IOHANNA BEVERLAI MONACA ME FECIT embroidered in black silk on the back have now largely decayed.

Girdle	Thick cord of silk, linen or cotton, often tablet woven with tassel ends, worn by all clergy as a symbol of holy purity. Originally used to tie back the alb when walking or working. Costly girdles decorated with silver often appear in wills. A tablet woven girdle of red silk was recovered from the tomb of Edmund Rich, Archbishop of Canterbury (1170-1240) and dates from the translation of the relics in 1247.
Heraldry	A system of signs and symbols, embroidered on surcoat, horse trappings and banners and often included a protecting saint and signs of the zodiac. They resulted from heightened interest in the Crusades, chivalry and the need for quick recognition on the field. There was a strong bias towards military figures in the designs, St Maurice the Roman centurian, St Martin the soldier bishop and St George overcoming the dragon. Saints are often dressed in armour in biblical scenes, soldiers around the cross in crucifixion scenes, with inscriptions to ward off danger. Influenced by Byzantine techniques and stitches, using brighter and more varied colours.
Gloves	Called manica meaning wristlet or cuff, and based on Greek word chirotheca or 'hand-case'. Bishops started wearing white or undyed silk gloves as an emblem of purity and an insignia of rank, as early as the seventh century. They were worn with the mitre and taken off when the bishop went to the altar to consecrate the bread and wine. The *Ordo Romanus* XI of 1271 maintained they should be the same colour as the bishop's chasuble or cope, blue, purple, rose, green, with white or red used most frequently for solomn episcopal functions, never black. Gloves had rings embroidered on the fingers; the bishop's actual ring was worn outside of the glove.
Hood	Changed from being a proper hood to small token triangular shape. It then became a large, rather clumsy hood, outlined with fringe and attached to the lower edge of the orphrey reaching halfway down the back of the wearer. The hood was also worn with a surplice, a sign of an academic degree.
Maniple, fanon	Developed from the *sudarium* or towel used by the priest. The embroidered strip of fabric 6 cm wide hung from the priest's or deacon's left wrist. The John the Baptist maniple was one of the great finds in the tomb of St Cuthbert. Both maniple and stole were originally made for Frithestan, Bishop of Winchester (909-31) on the orders of Queen Aelfflaed (died 916) and were later

given to St Cuthbert's shrine by King Aethelstan. The tomb was despoilt by Henry VIII's men in 1539-40, but in 1827 the grave was opened and the body was found within three coffins, still wrapped in precious Byzantine silks and rich textiles.

Mitre	Worn since the seventh century by bishops and archbishops. Began as a round cap, until the twelfth century when the two peaks were joined and embroidered lappets added to the back. It was then adopted with the gloves as part of the bishop's processional insignia, a sign of temporal power rather than any liturgical significance. Thomas Becket's mitre, embroidered in silver gilt thread on white silk, was presented to Cardinal Wiseman at Westminster Cathedral by the Archbishop of Sens and is now on loan to the V & A.
Morse	Fastening at the front of a cope, often highly decorated with embroidery, rare stones and filigree work.
Order of the Garter	Founded in 1340's by Edward III. John of Cologne made the first garters of blue taffeta embroidered in gold and silk with the motto *Hony soyt qe mal y pense*. He went on to design many garters, ornamental flags, bed-hangings and horse coverings.
Orifammes	Small sheer silk banners carried by ladies. The design can be clearly seen on both sides, embroidered with the Virgin Mary or a likeness of themselves. They developed into a special form of embroidery known as '*a deux endroit*'.
Orphreys	From *auriphryium* the Latin for gold embroidery. Originally just a decorative strip placed to hide the central seam down both front and back of the chasuble or the front edge of the cope. They were made from rich contrasting materials or elaborately embroidered with saints or religious scenes. Some orphreys were cross shaped, some just a central pillar. The John of Thanet orphrey has a dark blue silk twill background, sprinkled rampant lions, with an enthroned figure of Christ giving a blessing and holding the orb of the world.
Palls	Richly decorated coffin covers, often fringed and embroidered with patron saints and motifs relating to the particular Guild.
Pallium	Strip of folded white wool, worn over the shoulder, forming a Y-shape, decorated with black crosses. It was the insignia of an archbishop, a personal gift from the Pope, emphasizing allegiance to Rome rather than the Church and State in England.

Reliquary	Decorated silk or velvet bag made to hold a precious sacred item. A testament dated 1415 records that Henry Lord de Scrope bequeathed a little bag with a fragment of the true cross which he used to wear around his neck.
Rochet	A white linen garment worn only by the bishop and archbishop. It was similar to an alb with full sleeves drawn into a wrist band forming a ruff.
Scarf	A black broad piece of material, usually silk, worn around the neck and hanging straight down in front, part of the choir dress of the clergy.
Seal bags	Made to hold the seals attached to major documents. The Great Seal was attached to two charters dated 8th June 1319. The first is the Confirmation by Edward II of articles of better government of the City of London, and the second seal bag protects the seal of the Grant of the full use of the liberties to the citizens of London, both embroidered in coloured silks and silver gilt thread.
Stole or orarium	Worn by priests and deacons, ended in a fringe and was made in the same colour and material as the chasuble, dalmatic or orphreys. In 820 Amalarius, sometime Bishop of Trier maintained in *De Ecclesiasticis Officiis* that the stole 'symbolized the light yoke of Christ'.
Suit	A set of vestments. One set belonged to Archbishop Robert of Winchelsea (1294-1313). It was of red samite, embroidered with golden trees or branches with the orphreys worked with pearls. It included a cope, tunicle, dalmatic for the Archbishop and a second tunicle and dalmatic for the subdeacon and deacon. By 1400 Christ Church Canterbury had 96 copes with five chasubles, six tunicles, two dalmatics, 76 albs with stoles and fanons.
Surplice	Long flowing over-garment with long wide sleeves made of white linen.
Tunicle	Similar to the alb and dalmatic with simpler and slightly different ornamentation. It was made of plain fabric, shorter and narrower with side slits and worn under the dalmatic and chasuble by a subdeacon. A black tunicle, in the 1315-16 inventory of Canterbury, is embroidered with stars and golden beasts in circles, formerly belonging to Lanfranc.
Veil	Piece of white linen to cover the chalice.

Silk Glossary

Aglet, Aigulet, Aiglet	The metal tag called a 'point' on the end of a lace or cord.
Ailanthus	American breed of wild silkworm, where the silk is harvested.
Alamode	A thin light glossy black silk.
Anaphe	Wild silk from Africa, Uganda, Botswana. Silkworms feed on fig leaves and construct large nests containing clusters of cocoons.
Antheraea mylitta	A wild silkworm that feeds on the leaves of the jujube tree in India and spins large compact silver-gray cocoons.
Antheraea assama	Semi-domesticated wild silkworm from Assam.
Antheraea peryni	A wild tussah silkworm, native of Mongolia and Northern China. Since the disastrous pebrine epidemic in the mid 19th century, it has been found in the US, Spain and the Balearic Islands. It feeds on oak leaves and the silk is exported all over the world.
Antheraea Yamamai	Wild silkworm from Japan, produces large bright green cocoons with a strong white filament.
Antioch silk	General name for a rich brocaded silk cloth, woven in a number of places around the Mediterranean. Antioch in Syria was famous during the 10th to 12th centuries as a textile market. It sometimes features roundels with animals and birds whose heads, beaks and feet are highlighted in gold thread.
Antung	A Chinese silk fabric.
Arras	A rich tapestry fabric, mostly wool but silk is sometimes used for the fine accents, faces etc.
Arrindi	Wild silk from the Philosamia cynthia silkworm.
Attacas Atlas	Wild silkmoth from Northern India called Fagara. It has one of the largest wingspans, up to 25 cm and is found throughout Java, India, Sri Lanka, Burma and China.
Baldachin, baldaquin	A rich silk and gold canopy, originally a rich patterned silk from Baghdad.

Bale	A variable weight made up from books of silk. Chinese and Japanese bales of silk weigh between 55-65kg (125-140lbs). Italian bales weigh 90kg (200 lbs).
Barbette, gorget	A silk or linen cloth or band that covered the neck and sometimes part of the chest. It passed under the chin and was drawn up and pinned on the top of the head, the ends covered by the veil.
Batiste	Fine plain weave cloth of silk or cotton named after the French 13th century weaver and inventor Batiste Chambrai.
Batting	Thick layer of fluffy silk used for quilting and insulation in quilts and jackets.
Baudekin	A silk cloth with a warp of gold thread.
Baves	The twin fibres reeled off the cocoon together with the sericin gum.
Bell	A pack of c30 mawata caps made up of layers of broken cocoons stretched over a porcelain, bell-shaped frame. Caps are used in quilting, spinning, embroidery, felting and paper.
Bengaline	Silk fabric, silk warp with weft rib of cotton or wool.
Bisu	Husks of the cocoons left in the basin after reeling.
Bliaut	A man's garment worn with armour or at court, or a woman's dress.
Blaze	Short fuzzy fibres on the outside of the cocoons.
Bodhisattva	Buddhist saint or semi-divine personage.
Bombazine	Nineteenth century black twill weave silk fashionable for mourning clothes, often a half silk with wool or cotton.
Bombyx mori	Domesticated silkmoth, lays between 350 and 600 eggs, feeds on mulberry leaves. Silkworms produce white or pastel coloured cocoons, the basis for most of the world's silk production. The colour is in the sericin and washes out to leave white silk fibre.
Book of silk	A parcel of silk hanks weighing 2 kgs. Japanese silks were packed in books of 25-30 skeins. In the eighteenth century the guideline was 3000 cocoons make one book.
Bouchon	Rough knobs or loops on the surface of the silk threads.

Bouclé	A yarn with one or more looped threads plied with or onto the core yarn. In a woven fabric, the bouclé texture is achieved through using a looped or metallic secondary yarn in the weft.
Boulting cloth	A raw silk cloth with an open mesh texture used for silk screening or as a basis for embroidery. The warp is high twist organzine and the weft is held in place with the natural silk gum sericin.
Bourette	From the French *bourre se soie*, meaning floss or waste silk. A dull rough textured yarn or fabric, made from the very short waste fibres, including the crushed chrysalides and the final moulted skin of the silkworm. It has a cotton-like look and texture, shrinks initially but washes and takes the dye very well.
Bourrelet	A padded roll, added to or part of some medieval headdresses.
Braiding	A narrow flat woven edging or cord.
Braies	Outer linen short trousers worn by peasants and labourers and also short under-drawers.
Brigandine	Silk brocade or velvet with a small repeating pattern of circles or dots enclosing a star.
Brin	A single filament of liquid silk extruded by the silkworm through each spinneret and protected by the sericin or gum. The silk fibre hardens on contact with the air. Together two brins make a bave.
Brocade	Rich compound weave fabric utilizing various ground patterns, satin in the West, twill in Japan. The pattern is made using separate shuttles of different coloured silks or metallic yarns, to give a very rich patterned effect. Initially it required hand manipulation or the use of a drawboy who sat above the loom pulling the warp threads to a set pattern. Mostly now done on a mechanical or computerized jacquard loom.
Brocarts	A fabric heavily interwoven with gold and silver threads.
Brocatelle	Furnishing silk, similar to a damask weave, usually only one or two colours, with a satin or twill figure on a satin ground. The double warp ensures that the pattern lies proud or raised above the background.
Broché	A fabric with added richness through the use of additional warp yarns.

Calendering	A machine with heated rollers that impress the cloth with a moiré or watered effect.
Camlets	Originally a light rich fabric of silk and camelhair.
Camoca	A rich silk fabric.
Cannele	A weave with a ribbed surface formed by warp floats.
Carding	A process to straighten out or tidy loose or matted fibres preparatory to spinning. The fibres are drawn between rollers or wooden panels covered with a carding cloth of hooked wires.
Caul	Fitted cap.
Cendal	Silk fabric, often used for covering books.
Chaperon	Hood to cover the head and shoulders, worn by both men and women. It often ended with a long trailing point, called a liripipe. Later the shoulder section was lifted to form a hat, and the liripipe wrapped around to secure it.
Charmeuse	Fine silk satin fabric often used for lingerie.
Cheklaton	A costly silk with knots embroidered on it.
Chemise	General term for a fine silk or linen underdress, later an undergarment.
Chemisette	Fine silk cloth used to wrap a precious book or icon, with tassels on all four corners for carrying.
Chenille	From the French for a velvet or tufted yarn, originally silk.
Chiffon	From the French *chiffon* meaning a rag. A fine matt gauzy semi-transparent fabric made of high twist silk yarns, with a wide sett on the loom. In the 1920s, plain weave alternated with velvet pile sections, and was called crepe georgette. Voile, organdie and grenadine are similar fabrics, using different weight silk.
China silk	Light weight plain weave silk used for linings.
Chinoiserie	European designs imitated or inspired by Chinese patterns.
Chirimen	Expensive, heavy, crepe silk, used in Japan for Kimono, usually plain weave, sometimes with a woven pattern.

Chrysalis, pupa	The third stage of the development of the silkworm. After the silkworm has spun its cocoon it shrinks and forms a small brown shell within which the silkmoth develops.
Cloqué	From the French meaning a blistered surface. The crinkled effect comes from using a tightly twisted crepe yarn with a smooth filament thread.
Cloud-band	A band of pattern imitating a ribbon, sometimes with little scrolls along the edges, widely adopted during the Mongol period in China.
Cloth of gold	An elaborate, woven silk fabric heavily enriched with gold, in warp or weft.
Cocoon	Protective shell made up of fibre spun by the silkworm.
Coif	Tightly fitting linen cap with a chin strap, worn under the helmet, or for general wear by men and women.
Combing	A secondary process after carding to further refine and line up the fibres in preparation for spinning.
Compound weave	A complex weave incorporating two or more sets of warp or weft threads, so one set appears on the face and the other on the reverse, eg damask, brocade.
Corvée	Forced labour demanded by the state.
Cote/Cotte	A long dress or gown with long tight sleeves, worn by both men and women over a chemise and under a surcoat.
Cote-hardie	Originally worn over the gipon, ie a doublet, or super tunic. It was low necked and tight fitting over the hips, buttoned down the front, shorter for men and full-length for women. The edge was often dagged, sleeves were tight but sometimes flared out at the elbow. Tippets sometimes hung from a band around the upper sleeve. A high collar became fashionable after 1375.
Cordonnet	A waste silk, lightly spun, used for fringes and lacemaking.
Couching	A method of attaching threads, often silk, gold and silver to the surface of the textile, by over-sewing.
Count	The comparative thickness of a yarn expressed as the length of that yarn to a fixed weight.

Couvre-chef	Plain linen head scarf, usually worn by peasants and working women.
Crape	A stiff dull silk, usually dyed black, fashionable for 19th century mourning clothes.
Crêpe	A variety of weights of fabrics made up of tightly twisted yarn with two pairs of untwisted singles, one pair twisted 60-85 turns per inch in S direction, the other pair 60-85 turns per inch in Z direction, both pairs are twisted around each other with 5 S turns. All crêpe fabrics are degummed after weaving giving a very flexible fabric with a soft drape and dull matt finish. Variations include *crêpe de chine, marocain, crêpe georgette.*
Customary Law	Law based on accepted local or traditional values.
Cyclas	A rich purple fabric.
Dagging, Cut work	Fanciful way of decorating the edges of fabric during the 14th-15th centuries, by cutting or dagging the edges to form leaves, etc.
Damask	A single colour, figured, compound weave fabric with a flat, reversible design, combining warp and weft faced satin or twill weaves, possibly taking its name from the Syrian city of Damascus. According to Procopius in the 6th century, damask was woven in Tyrus, Antioch and Berytus, but no mention of Damascus. *Drap de damas de Lucchese* was frequently mentioned in inventories from 1350 onwards, but by the 15th century, Venice and Florence had become important silk centres with their own special designs incorporating fruit and flowers. By the 16th century, French and Spanish looms were making large patterned damasks, with oriental influence of palmettes, lotus flowers, crowns, meanders and pomegranates.
Degumming	The removal of the gum or sericin from the silk using a hot water bath with a soap or alkaline solution. It can be done either in the thread or after the fabric has been woven.
Denier	The comparative thickness of a filament yarn, thread or fibre expressed as the weight in grams to a fixed length of 9,000 metres. The *Association Internationale de la Soie* defines a denier as the weight in demi-decigrams of 450 m of silk, the smaller the number the finer the weight of silk.
Dtex	The weight in grams of 10,000 metres of silk thread or yarn.
Diapered	Checkered or diamond hatched background.

Diapause	A form of hibernation which allows the chrysalis or pupa to lie dormant over winter.
Diocletian Edict	3rd century sumptuary laws issued by the Emperor Gaius Diocletian in regard to wearing silk clothes, tailoring and weaving silk.
Dorelet	A hairnet embroidered with jewels.
Doublet	Short male upper garment, often quilted with two or more layers, originally an undergarment but soon became an outer garment like a vest or waistcoat with sleeves, worn with hose.
Doubling, plying, folding	Twisting together of two or more threads, usually in the opposite direction to form a stable yarn.
Douppion, Duppioni,	Originally meaning two cocoons, a medium weight slubbed silk fabric made from cocoons that have fused together in the course of being spun by the silkworms. This made it impossible to reel off the silk from the cocoon as a single filament, so they were spun separately. Fabric often handwoven using two colours, a thinner warp in one colour with a slubby weft in another, giving a shot silk effect.
Drawing, drafting	The process whereby fibres are gently drawn out from the mass or roving so that an even amount can be spun together to form a thread.
Duchesse satin	Heavy bridal or ceremonial weight satin.
Ecru	Natural coloured tussah silk thrown or woven before being degummed.
Ell	An old measure for fabric, measuring approximately 45 inches or 1.15m in England but varied in other countries.
Eri ailanthus	Wild silk moth, native of Bengal, Assam and Arrindi. Polyvoltine species including Philosamia ricini and Philosomia cynthia, producing up to seven generations each year. They feed on castor oil plants and produce loose flossy cocoons, orange-red or white. Neither can be reeled but must be spun and nowadays both are cultivated indoors.
Faconne	A figured silk fabric, often embellished with small ornaments.
Fagara	Silk produced from the Atlas moth, Attacus atlas.
Faille	A thick soft taffeta-style silk fabric, sometimes ribbed like a fine grosgrain, or given a moiré finish.

Fardel, torsello	A long canvas covered bale or bundle of skeined, raw or woven silk, a quarter of the weight that an animal can carry in each pannier bag. The emblem of the Lucchesse silk merchants and the Court of the Merchants.
Felt	A non-woven fabric where the fibres are bonded together by the action of heat, damp and pressure.
Ferronerie	A decorative curved design reminiscent of wrought iron work, often voided on velvet.
Feudalism	Theoretical structuring of society on the basis of a hierarchy with mutual obligations.
Fibres	Any long fine matter, natural or man-made that when laid together and twisted, can form a flexible yarn or thread.
Fibrillae	Specks on the surface of the yarn.
Fibroin	The protein based liquid silk that the silkworm ejects from its spinnerets when spinning its cocoon. It hardens on exposure to air to form silk fibre.
Fibula	A clasp or brooch.
Fief	A portion of land allocated to a knight to allow him to maintain himself and his household. As it was a gift it had service obligations to a higher authority.
Figured silks	The design is woven into the fabric, rather than embroidered on it.
Filament	Any continuous thread or fibre, natural or man-made.
Filature	The factory or community-based centre where silk cocoons are boiled and the silk reeled.
Filé	A smooth thread composed of a core of silk or linen thread with another metallic or gilded membrane wound around it.
Float	The weft or warp yarn carried over the surface of two or more threads of the weaving.
Floss, Frisons	The short irregular lengths of silk fibre taken off the cocoon before the single filament is reeled, usually lightly twisted and used in embroidery.

Flyer	An attachment to a spinning wheel or machine that allows the spun fibres to be wound and spaced on the reel automatically.
Foulard	A light-weight, woven twill silk, used for ties and scarves.
Friar	Male member of a Christian preaching order, rather than an enclosed monastic order.
Frontlet	15th century, a band of cloth, silk or velvet worn across the forehead.
Fuji	A firmly woven, medium-weight matt silk, easy to dye and work.
Fusarole	The round disc on a spindle used to weight it to keep the spindle spinning.
Galloon	Silk or metallic braid or ribbon used to trim uniforms, hats, upholstery.
Gauze, gaze, Gazzatum	A very fine sheer stiffened silk, often used for millinery, popular in Paris in the early 17th century, said to have come originally from Gaza.
Georgette	A soft semi-transparent silk, woven from tightly twisted two- or three-ply yarns making it feel a little stiffer than chiffon. Two untwisted singles combined with very hard twist 70-75 turns per inch either S or Z twist, giving a fine, strong, elastic yarn.
Gilded membrane, Parchment	Flat gilded strips, woven or embroidered into garments, fashionable in China during the Mongol period.
Gold thread	Wafer thin beaten gold wrapped around a silk core. After the Middle Ages, pure gold thread was usually replaced with silver gilt.
Grain	Smallest unit of weight being 1/5,760th pound (Troy) or 1/7,000th pound (*avoirdupois*). Dates from 1542 and was the weight of the centre of an ear of corn, used formerly as a measurement for cotton and linen. Also used to denote the horizontal and vertical line or lay of the fabric.
Graine	French term for silkworm seed.
Great Wardrobe	The section of a royal medieval household that dealt with clothing and textiles, furnishings, dry goods, spices, candles etc.

Green cocoons	Fresh, undried cocoons.
Grenadine	A very fine silk and/or woollen dress fabric, made from highly twisted organzine silk, possibly originally from Grenada in Spain.
Grise	The gray fur of the Russian squirrel.
Grosgrain	Plain silk with a heavy weft rib.
Ground	Background of the design or pattern.
Grisaille	Coloured in gray tones, with touches of colour in the faces and hands, known as *blanc et de noir*, white and black, sometimes used in stained glass and illuminated manuscripts.
Grotesque	Fanciful or fantastic human and animal forms often interwoven with foliage. Used as decoration in the initials or borders of medieval manuscripts.
Guild	An association of craftsmen and women in a particular trade, with rules and standards, usually requiring an apprenticeship for entry.
Gum, sericin	Gummy substance which causes the silk filaments to cling together when they are extruded through the spinnerets of the silkworm. Needs to be removed by being softened in hot soapy or alkaline water.
Gynaeceum	Women's weaving quarters during the Roman and Byzantium period but later not exclusively for women.
Habutai, Habutae	Plain woven lightweight silk, popular for scarves and linings.
Haincelin	A short houppelande, or outer gown, named after Haincelin Coq, a court jester to Charles VI of France, (1368-1422).
Hank	Skein of silk taken from the reel, tied in a number of places and twisted into a figure of eight.
Hantoug	A fairly inexpensive plain weave Chinese wild silk. The faintly pinkish look comes from the sericin or gum, and cannot be completely removed.
Hard spin	Fibres with a great number of twists to the inch.
Hard ply	Two tightly spun threads, tightly plied together, usually in the same direction.

Heraldry	A system of signs and symbols used to recognise aristocratic families, states, friends or foe in battle, tournaments, etc.
Heugue	A male outer gown, sleeveless and open at the sides, sometimes lined with fur, 15th century.
Holosericum	A Roman garment made entirely from silk.
Honan, Hunan	Handwoven Chinese silk fabric made from a combination of a wild tussah silk weft and domesticated Bombyx mori silk warp. It is a creamy colour and dyes in a subtle way because the dye takes differently on the tussah and bombyx mori silk fibres.
Houppelande	A characteristic garment from around 1380-1450, later known as the gown. It fitted on the shoulders, sometimes worn with a belt at the waist or hips, which formed the fullness into radiating pleats. Variations included extremely wide sleeves, dagged edges and a high upright collar, reaching to the ears. The length varied. Men's houppelande was long, knee length or very short with a front opening. The woman's was full length and closed at the front.
Icon	A painted devotional image of a saint, widely seen in the Orthodox Church.
Ikat	An Indonesian method of planned tie-dyeing of yarn in the skein before weaving to produce patterns in the warp and weft after they are woven. Also known as *chiné* by the French or *ébru* in Turkish.
Jacquard	A method of intricate decorative weaving using a string of punched cards in sequence. It was named after the discoverer, Joseph-Marie Jacquard, born in Lyons in 1752.
Jaque	A fitted jerkin, longer than a doublet, reaching nearly to the knee and buttoned in front.
Journeyman	A man or woman who had completed their years of apprenticeship plus a year and a day, now qualified and free to work for wages, or on their own account.
Khan	Supreme ruler in Turkish or Mongol States. Also a hostel used by merchants or travellers in Moslem countries.
Kincob	Metal brocade of Persian or Indian origin and a speciality of Benares. Chin in Chinese means gold.
Kirtle	A general name for a woman's gown or apron, of Saxon origin.

Lace	A tie to attach a sleeve, or hose.
	Also an open, decorative textile, made by manipulating the threads.
Lamé	Cloth where most of the pattern is made up of gold or silver threads.
Lampas or diasprum	A rich figured textile where supplementary warp and/or weft threads are added to the base fabric. The pattern is formed by the weft floats which are woven into the main ground. When these coloured threads are not required they are carried at the back.
Lapis lazuli	A semi-precious stone, available from remote mines in Afghanistan. When powdered produces the finest deepest blue pigment, ultra-marine.
Livery	A distinctive set of garments indicating that the person belongs to a particular household or guild.
Lustre	The reflection of light from the surface of the fibre or yarn, directly proportional to the straightness of the fibres and the tightness or looseness of the spinning and plying. Lustre is reduced by an uneven fibre surface.
Manichaeanism	A duelist religion of Persian origin, based on the teaching of Manes (c216-276), focusing on the conflict between light and dark. Had Christian, Gnostic and pagan elements.
Mantle	A loose outer garment worn by both men and women. Originally it was semicircular, open at the front and caught on the shoulder or at the centre front with a brooch.
Mantua	Possibly derived from the French word *manteau* meaning a silk gown or petticoat or Mantua in Italy.
Marquisette	Very sheer gauze weave.
Matelassé	From the French word meaning quilted, stuffed or padded. This medium weight silk was originally of two layers woven together. Now usually an embossed pattern, similar to cloqué.
Matka	Plain weave tussah fabric.
Mawata	Caps or handkerchiefs, made from cocoons where the moth has emerged, thereby breaking the threads. After boiling to dissolve the sericin they are stretched over a frame like a felt-hat steamer, the handkerchief is stretched between four pins. Most caps contain between 8 and 15 layers of cocoons, and 20-30 caps make a bell.
Mercer	A dealer in silks and other textiles.

Micron	One-thousanth of a millimetre, often written as u (pronounced mew). 1 micron = 1/25,400th inch.
Moches	A bale of imported raw silk.
Moiré	Silk taffeta fabric sometimes with heavier weft ribs. It has been drawn through heated and ridged rollers, which imprint a wavy pattern, also faille or *poult de soie*, or *moiré d'Angleterre*.
Momme	Abbreviated to mm. A Japanese unit of weight equivalent to 3.756 gms denoting the weight and fineness of a given woven silk.
Monovoltine	The silkworm species that produces one generation per year.
Moriculture	The cultivation of mulberry orchards.
Mousseline	Very lightweight silk.
Muga	The wild silk from Northern India and the province of Assam, produced by the silk moth Antheraea assanensis. It is soft and fine with a brilliant lustre.
Multivoltine	Silk worm species that produce a number of generations each year.
Nib	A lump of raw silk, formed by the collection of waste as a result of boiling the cocoons.
Noil	The very short, rough, knotty bits of silk, the final discard from carding, often containing black flecks from the last moulting of the silkworm's skin. It makes a dull yarn but weaves into a very hardwearing fabric that washes and takes the dye well. Usually piece dyed, colour can fade.
Opus Anglicanum	English work, rich, pictorial, ecclesiastical Medieval silk embroidery made in England between 900 AD and 1500 AD, featuring fine underside and surface couching, split stitch, goldwork, sometimes embossed with small gems.
Organza	A sheer, stiff, dull finished silk fabric, dyed in the yarn before the gum is removed. Sometimes extra chemicals are added to weight it, used in millinery and the couture industry.
Organzine	Fine high twist filament silk yarn, used for the warp. Two or more singles each having 16 S turns per inch then combined in opposite Z twist 12-20 turns.

Ottoman	A heavy plain silk with a finer warp and thick lightly twisted tram weft, giving a ribbed effect.
Paj	Chinese light-weight habutai woven silk, 20-24 grams or 5 to 8 momme.
Paltock	A jacket or gipon, introduced from Spain during the reign of Edward III.
Pattens	Wooden outer clogs or shoes held by a strap over the instep. Worn outdoors to protect footed fabric hose.
Pamphile	The daughter of Plateus, said to be the first person on the Greek Island of Cos to spin silk.
Passementarie	A French term for braids, tassels and trimmings.
Pile weave	Furry surface to the fabric made by extra warp or weft threads, later cut, as in velvet and corduroy.
Plaiting	A flat braid or cord with diagonal interlacing making a repeating pattern.
Points	The metal ends or ties for attaching hose, later referring to the whole tie or cord.
Poulaines, cracows	Long pointed shoes or boots, 14th-15th century.
Powdered	Sprinkled, as when a small flower or heraldic motif is scattered, embroidered or stencilled over the surface of the fabric.
Plying	The twisting together of two or more spun threads, usually in the opposite direction, to make a stable yarn.
Polyvoltine	Silkworm types that have many generations each year.
Pongée	Soft Chinese spun plain weave silk fabric, woven from tussah silk cocoons, easily washed, often used for blouses and summer garments. Pongee means 'handwoven' in Chinese, but it generally refers to a plain weave tussah fabric without slubs, machine or handwoven.
Pure silk	Silk without any added chemicals or other fibres.
Raw silk	Silk yarn or fabric with the gum or sericin still in it. This makes the silk look dull and retards the acceptance of dye, so it is usually removed by soaking in a very hot alkaline solution or soapy water.

Rayed	Fabric with diagonal stripes, popular in the 14th century.
Reeling	Drawing off or unwinding of the baves, or twin filaments, from a number of silk cocoons onto a large reel or wheel, the threads later thrown and wound into skeins.
Robe	A set of up to six matching garments, including tunics, mantles, cloaks. After the 1430s a robe refers to an outer sleeved garment worn by both men and women, a gown.
Roving	A soft and loosely held together rope of fibres with minimal twisting from which the spinner or machine draws out the fibres to the thinness required to spin the chosen yarn.
Samite	A weft faced compound twill, a heavy lustrous satiny silk fabric, frequently mentioned in medieval texts as being used for clothing, ceremonial garments, furnishings, funeral palls, occasionally patterned or interwoven with gold thread.
Sanguine	Scarlet.
Sarcenet	A fine light silk in plain or twill weave used for veils, said to have been made originally by the Saracens in Spain.
Samia cynthia	Wild silk moth which feeds on a variety of plants including the castor oil and Tree of Heaven (Ailanthus). It spins a very loose flossy cocoon, orange-red or white which cannot be unwound, and so is spun like wool or cotton.
Satin	A highly lustrous, smooth-faced silk fabric with a dull reverse, ranging from very light weight for use in lingerie to heavy duchesse satin for wedding gowns and furnishings. It is a twill based weave with five or more ends, the number of picks equal to or a multiple of the number of ends. The floating threads make it liable to snag.
Satin de Bruge	A half silk from the Netherlands made with silk and linen or worsted wool.
Satin stitch	Long smooth closely set embroidery stitch designed to cover the surface.
Schappe	A rather smelly system whereby the gum is removed from the silk by letting it ferment in water.
Scroop	The rustling sound made by weighted silk taffeta.

Seed, graine	Silkworm eggs.
Seint, Seynt	A girdle.
Sendal	Widely used strong, plain weave taffeta silk used for banners. Finer, lighter silk used for headdresses.
Sericin	A protective protein-based gum which keeps the two filaments together when they are extruded by the silkworm while spinning its cocoon. It makes up 25-30% of raw silk, and is removed by gentle boiling in soapy water or an alkaline solution.
Sericulture	The care and nurture of silkworms to produce cocoons and reelable silk.
Shantung	A northern province in China, known for its development of a tough, wearable, slubbed tussah silk fabric with a low lustre, heavier and rougher than pongee. Often the warp is made from the smooth Bombyx mori silk and the weft a slubby handspun tussah. Real shantung has a blue thread running down its selvedge and is only 33 inches (85 cm) wide.
Shot, Iridescent silk	Made by using one colour in the warp and another colour in the weft. This plain weave fabric catches the light, giving a constantly changing, sparkling effect with an iridescent sheen.
Siclaton	Silk cloth similar to Baudekin, 13th century.
Single gown	Unlined dress.
Singles	One thread, made up of 3-8 strands, twisted in one direction, loosely for weft, high twist for warp.
Sliver, rolag, tops	The loosely aligned and untwisted fibres prepared by carding, combing, or some mechanical means in preparation for spinning.
Sloppes	Meaning has changed from a jacket in the 14th century, to shoes or cassock in the 15th to breeches in the 16th century.
Slub silk	Soft loose knobs, the result of uneven spinning of the silk thread, can be in both warp and weft.
Soie grege	A dull raw untwisted silk, before it has been degummed
Spindle	A small smooth stick, weighted at one end. When the fibres are attached and the stick is twirled by the spinner, the fibres are drawn out and twisted together and form a thread. This thread is then wound onto the spindle shank.

Spinning	The process using a wheel, spindle or appropriate machine to draw out fibres and give them sufficient twist to hold together to form a single thread.
Silkworm Spinning	The process whereby a silkworm extrudes through two spinnerets on its head a continuous thread of liquid silk fibre which hardens on exposure to air and forms the cocoon.
Split stitch	A very fine medieval embroidery stitch where the lightly twisted silk is pierced at each stitch, used for finest detailing of faces, etc.
Spun silk	Short lengths of waste or non-filament silk which are carded, combed and spun to form a silk thread.
Stamped velvet	Velvet with a pattern stamped into it by feeding it through incised heated rollers.
Staple	Length of unspun fibres, measured in inches or centimetres.
Stencil	A method of imprinting a pattern on fabric, used by the Chinese and Japanese since 500AD.
Stifle	Method of killing the pupa or silkmoth by steam, heat or chemicals before it breaks through and emerges from the cocoon.
Sumptuary Law	Laws made to control what clothing or value of textiles various people in society could or could not wear.
Surah	A soft, glossy, heavier silk, often twill weave, used for ties, also known as foulard.
Surcoat	One of the set of garments that made up the Robe. It had very deep armholes which allowed the gown or cotte and girdle underneath to show through.
S-spin	Direction right to left in which fibres are spun to form a continuous thread.
Tabbi	Originally applied to striped silk, but later for silks with a wavy or watered appearance.
Tabby	Simplest weave, of alternating weft and warp threads, can be yarn or piece dyed, sometimes streaked or watered, a base for printed designs, said to come from Attabi, a textile producing area in Baghdad.

Taffeta	A plain weave silk, stiffened by the addition of metallic salts which cause it to rustle. Chemical treatments are now controlled because some are so harsh they rot the silk. Sometimes moiréd by pressing between two engraved rollers.
Taffeta impermeable	Oiled silk.
Tapestry	A method of weaving or embroidering a pattern to cover the surface, frequently pictorial or floral in design.
Tartar cloth	Silk from Tartary or old China. By the 14th century, term used to describe figured exotic silks patterned in gold with birds, animals and mythical beasts.
Tartaryn	An expensive cloth possibly of Chinese origin.
Textile	Any flexible cloth, plain or decorated, usually made from spun fibres through weaving, felting, knitting, lacemaking.
Thai silk	Traditionally a plain weave handwoven slubbed silk fabric, with brilliant colours, often with a shot silk effect.
Thread	Two or more single fibres twisted or plied together, usually in the opposite direction to the first spin.
Thread count	The number of warp or weft threads per unit to form a fabric.
Throwing	From the Anglo-Saxon word 'thrawn' meaning to twist. It is the second major process after reeling off groups of three to ten silk filament from the cocoons. This untwisted fibre is twisted and doubled together to make a more durable yarn.
Tippet	Long hanging streamer, like the liripipe on a chaperon or hood, or ties hanging from the headdress or upper arm of the cote-hardi.
Tiraz	Name both for the Moslem textile workshops and the woven bands made there, sometimes with Arabic writing woven into the fabric.
Tissage	French for weaving.
Tram	Thick, barely twisted silk fibres, used in the weft for filling to give a ribbed effect.
Tussah	The silk product of wild or undomesticated silkmoths, usually more ribbon-like in cross section and darker and coarser than Bombyx mori. Grown in the more temperate regions in the north of India, China, parts of Africa. It is the tannin in the leaves of the oak,

quercus, castor oil, bher tree etc., which gives the silk its distinctive creamy brown colour.

Tulle	A very fine netted silk, used for veils, decoration, millinery, named after the town of Tulle in France, where this invention was perfected.
Twill	A weave based on three or more ends and picks, offset to give a diagonal effect, used for surahs, herringbone and diamond patterns.
Velours	Tightly set napped silk. *Velours de Gene* is a polychrome floral voided Genoese velvet, not only made in Genoa. *Velours de Venise* and *Velours de Florence* are also velvets from Italy.
Velvet	A pile silk, of ancient origin, where extra warp threads form loops when they are laid over wires and later cut. They can be all pile, partly voided, of different heights to give a sculptural effect as in *alto-e-basso* or pile on pile velvet. Panné velvet results from irregular pressing. Some areas can be plain, satin or brocaded, metallic and gold threads used to heighten the design. In 1830, at Lyons, a new method was devised where two cloths were woven simultaneously, the loops joining them together. These were cut to separate the two fabrics, leaving both with a pile.
Voile	A fine silk woven with double or triple threads. Three untwisted singles combined with 30-40 S turns per inch.
Warp	Lengthwise threads laid on the loom.
Warp-faced cloth	Where additional warp threads are incorporated into the fabric so that the weft threads are completely covered.
Weft	The crosswise threads laid in between alternating warp threads to form the fabric, also called woof, picks, or filling threads.
Weft-faced cloth	Usually with a finer and closer set warp, and where the weft of filling yarns are packed down to completely cover the warp threads.
Wild silk	Undomesticated silk, including all the various coloured tussah style silks, Saturniidae giant silkworms, eri, muga, Attacus. The moths are generally much larger than the Bombyx mori, brown in colouring, and have an 'eye' on the wings.
Wimple	A veil covering neck and chin, worn by some married women during the middle ages.
Z-spin	The twist of fibres in spinning from left to right.

150

Bibliography

Abrams, Annie, "Women Traders in Medieval London", Economic Journal 26, (1916)

Alford, Lady, Needlework as Art, (Sampson, Low, Marston, Searle and Rivington, London, 1886)

Amt, Emilie, Women's Lives in Medieval Europe: A Source Book, ed. (Routledge, NY, London, 1993)

Anderson, Bonnie S & Judith P Zinsser, A History of their Own, Women in Europe from Prehistory to the Present, Vol 1. (Penguin Books, England, 1988)

Anquetil, Jacques, Soie en Occident, (Flammarion, Paris & New York, 1995)

Arano, Luisa Cogliati, The Medieval Health Handbook, Tacuinum Sanitatis, (George Braziller, NY, 1976)

Aruga, Hisao, Principles of Sericulture, Translated from the Japanese, (New Age International (P) Publishers, New Delhi, 2001)

Baer, Ann, Medieval Woman, Village Life in the Middle Ages, (Michael O'Mara Books, 1996)

Baines, Patricia, Spinning Wheels, Spinners and Spinning, (Batsford, London, 1991)

Baker, Derek, ed. Medieval Women, (Published for the Ecclesiastical Society by Basil Blackwell, Oxford, 1978)

Barham, Henry, An Essay Upon the Silkworm, 1719. Printed for Robin & Russ Handweavers, 1988.

Barron, Caroline, & Nigel Saul, England and the Low Countries in the Late Middle Ages, (Sutton Publishing, 1998)

Bautier, Robert-Henri, The Economic Development of Medieval Europe, (Thames & Hudson, London, 1971)

Bennett, H S, The Pastons and Their England, (Canto CUP, 1995)

Bennett, Judith M, et al, ed. Sisters and Workers in the Middle Ages, (The University of Chicago Press, Chicago & London, 1989)

Black, J Anderson, Madge Garland, and Frances Kennett, A History of Fashion, (Orbis, 1983)

Blake, E O, ed. Liber Eliensi, (Royal Historical Society, Camden Third Series 92 London, 1962)

Bolton, J L, The Medieval English Economy, 1150-1500, (Dent, London, 1988)

Bonavia, Judy, Sarah Jessup, & Edward Juanteguy, The Silk Road from Xi'an to Kashgar, (Passport Books, NTC Publishing Group, Lincolnswood, Ill. USA, 1993)

Boulnois, L, The Silk Road, Translated by Dennis Chamberlain, (George Allen & Unwin, London, 1966)

Bridenthal, R, Koomz, C, Stuard, S M, eds. Becoming Visible, Women in European History, 2nd ed, (Houghton Mifflin Company, Boston, 1987)

Bridgeman, Harriet & Elizabeth Drury, Needlework, An Illustrated History, (Paddington Press, NY & London, 1978)

Britnell, Richard, Daily Life in the Late Middle Ages, (Sutton Publishing, Stroud, Glos, 1998)

Bromley, John and Heather Child, The Armorial Bearings of the Guilds of London, (Frederick Warne & Co, London & New York, 1960)

Brooke, Iris, A History of English Costume, (Methuen, London, 1988)

Broudy, Eric, The Book of Looms, (Studio Vista, London, 1979)

Buckton, David, ed. Byzantium, Treasures of Byzantine Art & Culture, (Published for the Trustees of the British Museum, by the British Museum Press, 1994)

Cable, Mildred and Francesca French, Through the Jade Gate, (Constable & Co, London, 1932)
————The Gobi Desert, (Hodder & Stoughton, London, 1943)

Cansdale, C H C, Cocoon Silk, A Manual for those Employed in the Silk Industry and for Textile Students, (Sir Isaac Pitman & Sons Ltd, London, 1937)

Cantor, Norman F, Gen ed. The Pimlico Encyclopedia of the Middle Ages, (Pimlico, London, 1999)

Chan, Charis, The Odyssey Illustrated Guide to China, (Odyssey, 1994)

Christie, A G L, English Medieval Embroidery, (OUP, 1938)

Clark, Alice, Working Life of Women in the 17th Century, Economic Classics, Reprint, (Frank Cass & Co NY, 1968)

Clayre, Alasdair, The Heart of the Dragon, (Dragonbooks, 1985)

Corporation of London Record Office Journal, London, CLRO

Coss, Peter, The Lady in Medieval England, 1000-1500, (Sutton Publishing, 1998)

Cotterell, Arthur, The First Emperor of China, (Penguin Books, 1989)
————— The Pimlico Dictionary of Classical Mythologies, (London, 2000)

Crowfoot, Elisabeth, Frances Pritchard, & Kay Staniland, Textiles and Clothing c1150-1450, Medieval Finds from Excavations in London: 4, (Museum of London, HMSO, 1992)

Dale, M K, 'The London Silkwomen of the 15th Century' in The Economic History Review, No 4, 1932-34

D'Assailly, Gisele, Ages of Elegance, Five Thousand years of Fashion and Frivolity, (MacDonald, London, 1968)

Dean, Beryl, Ecclesiastical Embroidery, (Batsford, 1960)

Dixon, E, "Craftswomen of the Livre des metiers", Economic Journal 5, (1895)

Dollinger, Philippe, transl D S Ault & S H Steinberg, The German Hanse, (Macmillan, 1970)

Drege, Jean-Pierre and Emil M Buhrer, The Silk Road Saga, (Facts on File, New York, Oxford, 1989)

Duby, Georges, ed. A History of Private Life, II. Revelations of the Medieval World, (Harvard University Press, 1988)

Early Chancery Proceedings ECP

Ekwall, E, ed. Two Early London Subsidy Rolls, (Lund, 1951)

Ennen, Edith, The Medieval Woman, translated by Edmund Jephcott, (Basil Blackwell, Oxford, 1989)

Erler, Mary & Maryanne Kowaleski, Women & Power in the Middle Ages, (University of Georgia Press, 1988)

Evans, Joan, The Flowering of the Middle Ages, (Guild Publishing, London, 1985)

Fagan, Brian, New Treasurers of the Past, (Guild Publishing, London, 1988)

Fairbanks, John K and Edwin O Reischauer, China Tradition and Transformation, (George Allen and Unwin, London, Boston, 1979)

Feltwell, Dr John, The Story of Silk, (Alan Sutton, 1990)

Fitch, Marc, "London Makers of Opus Anglicanum" in Transactions of the London and Middlesex Archaeological Society No XXVII , (1976)

Franck, Irene M & David M Brownstone, The Silk Road, A History, (Facts on File, NY, 1986)

Gaddum, H T, Silk, (H T Gaddum & Co, Macclesfield, 1979)

Gies, Frances & Joseph, Women in the Middle Ages, The lives of Real Women in a Vibrant Age of Transition, (Perennia Library, Harper & Row NY, 1978)
————Merchants and Moneymen, The Commercial Revolution, 1000-1500, (Arthur Barker Ltd, London, 1972)

Ginsburg, Madeleine, Illustrated History of Textiles, (Studio Edition, 1991)

Goldberg, P J P, Women, Work and Life Cycle in a Medieval Economy, 1300-1520, (Claredon Press, Oxford, 1992)
————Women in Medieval English Society, (Sutton Publishing, 1997)

Gross, C , The Guild Merchants, Vol II, (OUP, 1927)

Hafter, Daryl M, ed. European Women and Preindustrial Craft, (Indiana University Press, Bloomington & Indianapolis, 1995)

Hali Publishing, Silk & Stone, The Art of Asia, (London, 1996)

Hallam, Elizabeth, ed. The Plantagenet Chronicles, (Colour Library Books, 1995)

Hanawalt, Barbara A, ed. Women and Work in Preindustiral Europe. (Indiana University Press, Bloomington, 1986)

Hao, Qian, Chen Heyi & Ru Suichu, Out of China's Earth, Archaelogical Discoveries in the People's Republic of China, (Frederick Muller Limited London and China Pictorial, Beijing)

Hedin, Sven, Through Asia, 2 vols, (Methuen, 1898)
————The Silk Road, (George Routledge & Sons, London, 1938)

Herlihy, David, Medieval Households, (Harvard University Press, 1985)

Holmes, George, ed. The Oxford Illustrated History of Medieval Europe, (BCA, 1992)

Houston, Mary G, Medieval Costume in England & France, 13th 14th and 15th centuries. (Dover Publications Inc, New York. 1996)

Howell, Martha C, Women, Production and Patriarchy in Late Medieval Cities, (University of Chicago Press, 1986)

Hufton, Olwen, The Prospect Before Her, A History of Women in Western Europe, Vol 1, 1500-1800, (Fontana Press, 1997)

Humble, Richard, Marco Polo, (Book Cub Associates, London, 1975)

Inalrik, Halil with Donald Qualaert, An Economic and Social History of the Ottoman Empire, 1300-1914, (1994)

Ingram, Elizabeth, ed., Threads of Gold, Embroideries and Textiles in York Minster, (Pitkin Pictorials, Andover, 1987)

Ivy, Jill, Embroideries at Durham Cathedral, (The Dean and Chapter of Durham Cathedral, 1992)

Jewell, Helen, Women in Medieval England, (MUP, 1996)

Jewett-Zworykin, Chambers Biographical Dictionary, 2 vols, (Chambers Paperback , Edinburgh, 1975)

Jones, Mary Eirwen, A History of Western Embroidery, (Studio Vista, London, 1969)

Kanner, Barbara, ed. The Women of England, From Anglo-Saxon Times to the Present, Interpretive Bibliological Essays, (Mansell, London, 1980)

Kemper, Rachel, H. A History of Costume, (Newsweek Books, NY, 1979)

Kendrick, A F, English Embroidery, (London, 1904)

King, Donald, Catalogue of Opus Anglicanum, Exhibition at the V&A, (Arts Council, London, 1963)

Kingsford, C L, ed. Stows Survey of London, (Oxford at the Clarendon Press, 1908)

Kirshner, Julius & Suzanne Wemple, Women of the Medieval World, Essays in Honour of John H Mundy. (Basil Blackwell, 1985)

Klapisch-Zuber, Christiane, Georges Duby, & Michelle Perrot, eds. A History of Women, Silences of the Middle Ages, (The Belknap Press of Harvard University Press, London, 1992)

Kock, Dr Ernst, Rule of St Benet, EETS, (Kegan Paul, London, 1902)

Kolander, Cheryl, A Silkworkers Notebook, (Interweave Press, 1985)

Labarge, Margaret Wade, Women in Medieval Life, (Hamish Hamilton, London, 1987)

Lacy, Kay " The Production of Narrowware by Silkwomen in 14th and 15th century England", Textile History Vol 18, No. 2, Autumn (1987)

Lattimore, Owen & Eleanor, Silks, Spices and Empire, seen through the eyes of its discoverers, The Great Explorers series, (Tandem Books, 1973)

Laver, James, A Concise History of Costume, World of Art Library, (Thames and Hudson, 1979)

Le Coq, Albert von, Buried Treasures of Chinese Turkestan, (Allen & Unwin, 1928)

Le Goff, Jacques, ed. The Medieval World, (Collins & Brown, London, 1990)

Leyser, Henrietta, Medieval Women, A Social History of Women in England, 450-1500 (Weidenfeld and Nicholson, London, 1995)

Liu, Xinru, Silk & Religion, An Exploration of the Material Life and the Thought of People. 600-1200, (OUP Dehli, 1996)

Lloyd, Sarah, Chinese Characters, A Journey through China, (Collins, 1987)

Lloyd, Simon, English Society and the Crusade 1216-1307, (Clarendon Press, Oxford, 1988)

Lopez, Robert S, and Erwin W Raymond, Trans and Eds. Medieval Trade in the Mediterranean World, NY n.d. Part of the Records of Civilization, Sources and Studies series

Mandeville, Sir John, The Travels of Sir John Mandeville, (Penguin Classics, 1983)

Marshall, Robert, Storm from the East, From Genghis Khan to Khublai Khan, (BBC Books, London, 1993)

Mayo, Janet, A History of Ecclesiastical Dress, (Batsford, London, 1984)

Miller, Edward and John Hatcher, Medieval England, Towns, Commerce and Crafts, 1086 - 1348. A Social and Economic History of England, (Longman, London & New York, 1995)

Mirsky, Jeannette, Sir Marc Aruel Stein, Archaeological Explorer, (Chicago, 1977)

Murowchick, Robert E, China, Cradle of Civilization, Ancient Culture, Modern Land, (University of Oklahoma Press, 1994)

McGuinness, Stephen & Mitsuri Uragami, Chinese Textile Masterpieces, Sung, Yuan and Ming Dynasties, Cat. Oct 25-Nov 3 1988 V&A

Nicolle, David, The Mongol Warlords, Genghiz Khan, Kublai Khan, Hulegu, Tamerlane, (Firebird Books, 1990)

Nunn, Joan, Fashion and Costume 1200-1980, (The Herbert Press, London, 1985)

Piponnier, Francoise & Perrine Mane, Dress in the Middle Ages, Transl. Caroline Beamish, (Yale University Press, New Haven and London, 2000)

Polo, Marco, The Travels of Marco Polo, Introduced by John Masefield, (Everyman's Library, Dent, London, 1975)

Power, Eileen, English Medieval Nunneries, c1275 to 1535, (Cambridge at the University Press, 1922)
——— Medieval People, (Methuen London, Barnes & Noble, New York, 1963)

Public Record Office PRO, London

Reischauer, Edwin and John K Fairbank, East Asia: The Great Tradition, (Houghton Mifflin, Boston, 1960)

Ribeiro, Aileen, Dress and Morality, (B T Batsford, London, 1986)

Reyerson, Katherine, "Medieval Silks in Montpelier, 1250-1350" Journal of European Economic History II (1982)

Riley H T, Transl. 'Liber Albus of the City of London, complied in 1410 by John Carpenter, Common Clerk and Richard Whittington, Mayor.' in Guildhall Studies in London History iii, 1861 (Richard Griffin & Co, 1978)

Riley-Smith, Louise & Jonathan, The Crusades, Idea and Reality 1095-1274, Documents in Medieval History 4, (Edward Arnold, London, 1981)

Saul, Nigel, The Age of Chivalry, Art & Society in Medieval England, (Brockhampton Press, 1995)

Scott, Margaret, The History of Dress Series, Late Gothic Europe 1400-1500, (Humanities Press, NJ. 1980)

Scott, Philippa, The Book of Silk, (Thames & Hudson, London, 1993)

Sharpe, R R ed. Calendar of Letter Books, Preserved among the Archives of the Corporation of the City of London, 1275-1498. Books A-L., (London, 1899-1912)

Sharpe, R R, ed. Calendar of Wills Proved and Enrolled in the Court of Hustings, London, 1258-1688, 2 vols, (London, 1889-90)

Simkin, C G F, The Traditonal Trade of Asia, (OUP, London, 1968)

Staniland, Kay, Embroiderers, Medieval Craftsmen, (British Museum Press, London, 1994)

Stark, Freya, The Valley of the Assassins and Other Persian Travels, (Century, London, 1936)

Stein, Marc Aurel, Ruins of Desert Cathay, A personal narrative of Explorations in Central Asia and Westernmost China. Two Volumes, (Dover Publications Inc, New York, 1912)

Sutton, Anne, "Alice Claver, Silkwoman" in Medieval London Widows, 1300-1500, Caroline Barron and Anne Sutton, (Hambledon Press, London, 1994)

Synge, Lanto, Antique Needlework, (1982)

Thomas A.H. (vols. 1-4) and P E Jones (vols. 5-6) Calendar of Plea and Memoranda Rolls Preserved among the Archives of the Corporation of the City of London, 1323-1482, 6 vols, (Cambridge University Press, 1926-61)

Thompson, A Hamilton, Bishop Alnwick's Visitation Records of Religious Houses in the Diocese of Lincoln, Vol II, Pt 1 & 2, (London, Canterbury & York Society, 1929)

Thrupp, Sylvia, The Merchant Class of Medieval London. (University of Michigan Press, Ann Arbor, 1962)

Toynabee, Arnold, ed. Half the World, The History and culture of China and Japan, (Thames and Hudson, London, 1973)

Tyerman, Christopher, England and the Crusades 1095-1588, (University of Chicago Press, Oxford, 1988)

Uitz, Erika, Women in the Medieval Town. (Barrie & Jenkins, London, 1990)
———— The Legend of Good Women, The Liberation of Women in Medieval Cities, (Moyer Bell, 1994)

Vaughan, Richard, trans & ed. The Illustrated Chronicles of Matthew Paris, (CUP, 1993)

Volbach, W Fritz, Early Decorative Textiles, (Paul Hamlyn, London, 1969)

Von Le Coq, Albert, Buried Treasures of Chinese Turkestan, (Oxford University Press, Hong Kong, Oxford, New York, 1985)

Walker, Anabelle, Marc Aurel Stein

Wallis, Penelope, 'London, Londoners and Opus Anglicanum', in The British Archaelogical Association Conference Transactions for the year 1984 X, Medieval Art, Architecture and Archaeology in London (1990), ed. Lindy Grant.

Warner, Pamela, Embroidery, A History. (Batsford, London, 1991)

Waters, Charlotte, An Economic History of England, (OUP London, 1947)

Watt, James, CY, & Anne Wardwell, When Silk was Gold, Central Asian and Chinese Textiles, (Abrams US, 2000)

Wensky, Margaret, "Women's Guilds in Cologne in the Later Middle Ages", Journal of European Economic History 11 (1982)

Willett, C & Phillis Cunnington, Handbook of English Mediaeval Costume, (Faber, 1952)

Williams, Marty & Anne Echols, Between Pit & Pedestal, Women in the Middle Ages, (Markus Wiener, New Jersey, 1994)

Yang, Sunny, Hanbok, The Art of Korean Clothing, (Holly M. 1997)

Yap, Yong & Arthur Cotterell, The Early Civilization of China, (BCA, London, 1975)

Index

For additional references
see Appendix

Silk historian and medievalist, Priscilla Lowry spends nine months of her year giving lectures and workshops in the UK, US and Canada. She travels to New Zealand to spend the summer at the beach with her family, taking the opportunity to visit colleagues, to write, do research and design and make the handspun and knitted silk garments featured in the fashion parades.